Sydney-based Debbie Malone, the 2013 Australian Psychic of the Year, is an acclaimed and highly respected psychic, clairvoyant, psychometry expert and spirit medium.

Debbie assists police to solve murder investigations and missing persons' cases. She conducts private readings and workshops on how to tune into the spirit world, and is regularly interviewed in national print and on television and radio. Television appearances include *Today Tonight, Sensing Murder, Sunrise, Today, The Project* and most recently *The One*.

Her extraordinary gift has enabled her to receive visions from both the living and the dead, from the past, present and future, and to convey messages to bereaved families from their departed loved ones. She also specialises in paranormal spirit photography.

Debbie's book *Never Alone: A Medium's Journey* was first published in 2009, followed by *Awaken Your Psychic Ability* in 2016.

Debbie has also created a series of bestselling *Angel cards* — *Angels Whisper* & *Angel Wishes Cards, Angels to Watch Over You* and *Angel Reading Cards*.

Debbie Malone's gift has enabled her to see beyond the here and now and she draws strength from using the world of spirit to help herself and others, and from knowing that we are never alone.

www.betweentwoworlds.net

CLUES FROM BEYOND

TRUE CRIME STORIES FROM **AUSTRALIA'S #1** PSYCHIC DETECTIVE

DEBBIE MALONE

ROCKPOOL
PUBLISHING

A Rockpool book
PO Box 252
Summer Hill
NSW 2130
Australia
www.rockpoolpublishing.com.au
http://www.facebook.com/RockpoolPublishing

First published in 2017
Copyright text © Debbie Malone 2017
This edition published in 2017

National Library of Australia Cataloguing-in-Publication entry

Creator: Malone, Debbie, author.
Clues from beyond / Debbie Malone.
9781925429473 (paperback)
Subjects: Women mediums--Australia--Anecdotes.
Parapsychology in criminal investigation.
Criminal investigation--Psychological aspects.
True crime stories.

Cover design by Seymour Design
Cover image by Pexels
Internal design by Jessica Le, Rockpool Publishing
Typeset by Graeme Jones
Printed and bound in Australia

10 9 8 7 6 5 4 3 2

CONTENTS

Introduction

Twenty-four years ago my life was changed forever. After experiencing six near-death experiences through illness and a miscarriage in 1992, I began to see dead people. I did see them as a child but I had managed to find a way to shut them out. Unfortunately, after the miscarriage, I had no control over the visions that I received on a nightly basis. The visions I saw were terrifying. I saw people being shot, stabbed, strangled, bashed, raped and set alight. The night became a time of fear, not a time of peace. I was frightened to go to sleep because these nightly events seemed to go on forever.

I began to question what I had done to deserve what I was going through. I tried everything to make the nightmares go away. The more fearful I became, the worse the visions were. At this time I was introduced to my living angel, Patricia McRae. Patricia is a gifted medium and reverend of the spiritualist church near where I live. It was through her help and guidance that I began to understand and realise that I had gone through a spiritual awakening. Instead of fearing my abilities, I began to embrace them and learn how to harness them to help those in the spirit world.

The life that I live now is nothing like I could have ever imagined. I have always been a creative and artistic person and my chosen vocation was graphic designer and photographer, not psychic medium.

To be honest, I would never have chosen my current line of work. I was not someone who would go and see psychics and I always lived with the motto of 'what you don't know doesn't hurt you'. It seems that the spirit world had other ideas.

This type of work comes with a huge responsibility and I take what I do very seriously. I feel that I must have been given this ability for a reason, and if I can help one person then my life's purpose is worthwhile. I wish to point out that as a psychic medium I do not solve cases. I am an investigative resource who can be utilised by police to pick up information that may provide new lines of inquiry in an unsolved crime.

I understand that not everyone will be accepting of what I do. It is not my business what others think of me. I am not here to change people's belief systems. However, I would like to open their minds to the possibility that life exists beyond the grave and give victims of crime a voice.

I feel blessed to have had the opportunity to meet and assist many talented police officers, who dedicate their lives to work on cold cases involving the missing and the murdered. I have been able to connect with the victims of many crimes to pass on clues and information.

This journey has been extremely challenging, stressful, dangerous, trying and testing. I am a psychic witness who hears the screams and experiences the pain, the fear, the terror and suffering of the victims while tuning in to each case. I hear and see what they experience during their time of death.

I can experience a crime through the victim's eyes, those of the murderer or as a silent witness watching as if I am actually at the crime scene.

I have been able to tune in to the victims by holding locks of their hair, bloody clothing, watches, jewellery, shoes and photographs to make a connection. At times this can be quite a confronting experience because every item contains the energy of the victim. Through this type of contact I am privy to the life that the victim lived before, during and after their death. I see visions of them, hear their words, see them as if they were still alive. I see signs and symbols, smell their perfume or that of vegetation where they are located. I can see the murderer's face and have worked with police artists to create 'comfits' and 'identikits' to identify the perpetrators I see.

At times this work has been a soul-searching experience that has made me question why I do what I do.

I have worked with police officers throughout Australia. Some have been open to my assistance while others have been very sceptical and negative. What has been most interesting is that some of the most sceptical officers have become believers and great friends.

My first book *Never Alone*, which was published in 2009, was about my personal journey from being the sceptic to becoming the psychic. It looked at a number of high-profile cases I worked on. Since its release I have continued to work on cold cases with the police.

The main aim of *Clues from Beyond* is to share the stories of some very special people. Some of them have been found and others are still missing. Each and every one of these people has touched and changed my life forever. Their stories are heartwrenching and at times horrifying. They all have families who love them dearly and it is important that one day their loved ones find out the truth about what happened to them.

Some of the victims featured in this book may never be found. However, it is important to know that they existed and that their story is told. I know that there are people out there who may have information about these crimes that could help the police. There are also perpetrators who know what they did — I hope that they have a conscience and come forward to allow the families closure.

If you do have any information concerning any of these cases, please contact Crimestoppers at: www.crimestoppers. com.au or phone 1800 333 000.

Chapter 1

Working with the Cadaver Dog Unit

I first met Dave Cole and Roger Mayer from the New South Wales Police Force Dog Unit while working on the Kay Docherty and Toni Maree Cavanagh case in Gerroa (see chapter 7). Since then I have worked on a number of cases with them, including the Kiesha Abrahams case.

NAME: Kiesha Abrahams

MISSING SINCE: 31 July 2010

LAST SEEN: Mount Druitt, NSW

DATE OF BIRTH: 22 April 2004

AGE AT DISAPPEARANCE: 6

GENDER: Female

BUILD: Slim

HAIR: Curly blonde/brown

EYES: Blue

CLOTHING: Last seen wearing pink pyjamas and purple Pumpkin Patch jacket

Kiesha Abrahams.
Source: Family

At 10.03 am on Sunday, 1 August 2010 Kristi Abrahams rang the police emergency number to report that her daughter Kiesha was missing. When Kristi woke up that morning, she noticed that her front door was open. Then she discovered Kiesha was gone. Kristi told the switchboard operator that her daughter was six years old, she was in her pyjamas and she had blonde hair and blue eyes.

Police were immediately dispatched to the family's home, an apartment in the western Sydney suburb of Mount Druitt. Kristi lived there with her partner Robert Smith and her two daughters, Kiesha and three-year-old Breeana.

◎　◎　◎

In 2010, I had a client book in for a reading. Unbeknown to me, the woman was a relative of a missing little girl named Kiesha Abrahams. (To protect my client's privacy, I have changed her name — I will call her Sharon.)

During the reading Sharon gave me a hot pink bucket hat with a picture of Dora the Explorer printed on the outside and the name 'Kiesha' written in black marker on the inside. I was also given a number of photographs to read.

From the moment I held the hat, I could feel the presence of a cheeky little girl energetically running around my room. The saddest part of doing this reading was that I could feel the energy of the little girl and I could see her in the room with us, which indicated that she was no longer alive.

One of the photographs was of Kiesha as a small child and she looked healthy and happy. I asked Sharon about the picture and she said it was taken when Kiesha was in foster care —

this explained why this image of Kiesha was so different to the other ones I held. Sharon said that unfortunately Kiesha was taken away from her foster family and placed back with her mother Kristi and her partner Robert Smith. Sharon was a loving relative of Keisha's who showed grave concerns for her safety. She hoped that by visiting me, she and other family members would be able to find out what happened to Kiesha after her disappearance.

I closed my eyes and held onto the hot pink bucket hat to see if I could fill in the missing pieces. Kiesha began to give me images of what her life was like while she was alive. As a mother of three, what I saw was quite distressing. The images and feelings I picked up from this tiny little girl were something I couldn't even begin to comprehend. I was shown images of violence towards her. She showed me that she was always in trouble with her mother and that her mother and stepfather would burn her on the arms and legs with their cigarettes as punishment. She told me that she always wore a hat because her mother pulled her by the hair and she had big clumps of hair missing from her head. I could see that she had bruises on most parts of her body at one time or another. I also saw that Kiesha wasn't fed properly. She showed me that she was often bought takeaway food such as McDonald's and given packets of potato chips, tiny teddies and other junk food to keep her quiet.

I asked Sharon if she could confirm the images that I was seeing. She said that she worried about the way the little girl was treated. Sharon had her own small children and she said that she liked to have Kiesha over to her home so that she could play with her own kids and be able to be a normal child.

The last time that she had seen Kiesha alive, Sharon said, was approximately two weeks before the girl was reported as missing. She said that Kiesha had been at one of her children's birthday party. She said that at the time Kiesha had clumps of hair missing, which she thought was distressing.

Sharon asked me if I thought Kiesha was dead or alive. The answer was very heartbreaking. The news that Kiesha was in spirit is not something anyone would want to hear. She asked what I thought had happened to Kiesha. This was another hard question to answer.

Sharon was a softly spoken woman who showed grave concerns for Kiesha. The love she expressed for her was very sincere. If only Kiesha had a mother like Sharon I am sure she would still be alive today.

We decided to focus on what had happened to the little girl and where she could be found. I asked Kiesha to tell me where she was. She showed me that she was in bushland and that she was near water. The water was like that of a small creek and I felt that it was in an area of western Sydney. I grew up in Blacktown and I felt that it was west of there. The area was in the proximity of Mount Druitt, St Mary's or possibly Penrith. I knew that it was not far from power lines — I could see electrical towers in the distance and I could smell dirt. I could also smell eucalyptus trees, which also confirmed that she was in bushland. She showed me that there were dirt tracks near where she was buried and that BMX bike and motor-cross riders rode their bikes past. I felt that she was confined in a large sports bag or a suitcase and I was picking up severe head injuries.

The room where I conduct my readings is painted blue and I have decorated it with angels and fairies. In one corner I have a large fairy tree. While I was conducting the reading, I could see Kiesha standing next to the tree and looking at all of the fairies. I told Sharon what I was seeing and how excited Kiesha was with all the fairies and the angels. Kiesha then gave me the image of a purple butterfly. When I asked Sharon if Kiesha liked fairies, her eyes lit up and she told me that Kiesha loved fairies and butterflies. Purple was Kiesha's favourite colour.

It was a lovely moment to change the subject and talk about something so heart-wrenching yet happy, instead of the horror we both knew that this poor little six-year-old girl had experienced.

The reading drew to a close and I asked Sharon if I could borrow Kiesha's hat and a photograph of her. I wanted to tune in further to see if I could pick up any more information over the next couple of days. Sharon agreed and we organised to keep in touch.

That night I was running a workshop in the main office area with a group of students who were coming to learn psychometry. I had left Kiesha's hat in the reading room with the photograph and shut the door during the workshop. When the class members were doing their exercises on how to tune in, a number of them could hear what sounded like someone whistling in my reading room. At first I thought that we were hearing things and then I decided to go into the room to see what was going on.

The whistling sound was even louder when I entered the room. All the students could hear it too. A few of us decided to echo the whistle back to whoever was making the sound. I thought that it could only be Kiesha because her belongings were still sitting on the sofa in the reading room. We whistled back the same tune that she was whistling and she whistled back. The sound was quite distinct — it was more like a child who was learning to whistle, more of sucking in air to make the whistling sound than of blowing out air to make the sound.

I grabbed my iPhone and recorded what was taking place and, at the same time, videoed with the phone light on, which is a way to capture any spirit energy if it is present. What I saw was quite incredible. The phone captured an orb that was moving back and forth between the hat and the fairy tree. As I whistled to Kiesha, the orb began to interact with me. It was lovely to see that even though little Kiesha had suffered so much horror in her life, in death she still had the sense of being a child in the spirit world. She was still as active and inquisitive as she was when she was alive. I felt that Kiesha was trying to give me a sign that she was happy with the work I was trying to do to assist her and her family member.

I decided to tune in to Kiesha further the following day. However, she had other ideas. While driving home, I felt that I had a new little friend in the car and began to realise just how connected Kiesha and I had become. To be honest, experiencing the pain and suffering of such a little child is extremely hard to cope with. The sense of loss really affects you. I could never even begin to imagine what it would be like to hurt or witness the assault on a child in any form. The anguish would multiply tenfold if it was a member of your own family.

I found it horrific that Kiesha's mother and stepfather were responsible for what subsequently caused her death. A mother is supposed to love, nurture and above all protect her child. It was so difficult to fathom what was going on in the minds of Kristi Abrahams and Robert Smith when they killed this tiny fragile little girl.

Settling down to go to sleep that night, I knew I wasn't alone. I could feel Kiesha's energy with me and I felt her get into bed and put her arms around me — all this tiny little girl wanted was to be loved. I lay in bed feeling her tiny arms around me and I didn't want to let her go. I told her that I would do all I could to try and help her so that she could go to heaven and be up among the angels. I told her that she was going to be safe and that she didn't have to suffer anymore.

When I finally fell asleep, I dreamed about Kiesha and her dreadful life. I could see her stepfather Robert and her mother Kristi yelling at her and I could see her cowering in the corner in fear of them both. I just couldn't believe what I was seeing. All the visions I saw were dreadful. I have worked on a number of cases that are connected to children and the images I received about what happened to Kiesha are some of the worst things I have ever witnessed.

I always wonder why bad things happen to innocent beings. People tell me it is karma, but surely there is no karma for a gorgeous six-year-old girl who is innocent, loving and just wanted to be loved. What is more to the point, I think, is that not all people deserve to be parents. Being a parent is the greatest gift of all and this should be honoured and respected and not taken for granted.

Kiesha began to show me her perspective on her life and on what her mother and stepfather had done to her. I was given psychic impressions that she may have been placed in a suitcase or large duffle bag and put in a garage or a shed area before she was buried. I was shown images as if I was inside a garage — the area was dark and I could see rolls of carpet and lots of discarded junk inside. The impression was as if she was just thrown away like rubbish. I felt that she had suffered from multiple traumas to the head and she told me she had a sore arm. It was as if someone had pulled and twisted it so hard that her arm was pulled out of its socket.

She showed me that she didn't like to smile because her teeth were all broken from being hit in the mouth. She told me that she got in trouble with her mother because she kept nagging to be allowed to go to school. Kiesha said that she liked going to school because there were other children to play with and she loved to learn new things. I also felt that she knew it was a safe place away from her parents. Her mother probably didn't send her there much because she feared that someone at the school would have been suspicious about the bruising, the loss of hair and the injuries she constantly had on her body.

I could see that Kiesha was a very busy girl who wanted to have lots of attention. I could see that she wasn't naughty — she was just a child who needed to be occupied and doing things. She showed me how she liked to draw and colour in and she disliked being stuck inside the house most of the time. Kiesha said that she was very excited that she had a little sister and she told me that her mummy was having a baby. She showed me the image of sitting on a sofa next to her mother and patting her tummy in anticipation of her new sibling arriving into the family.

I didn't have much sleep that night as the many visions and messages that Kiesha was showing me were floating through my head. I woke up extremely tired and sad with the knowledge that someone should have saved this little girl.

I rang Sharon and shared with her the information I had about Kiesha. I told her what Kiesha did at my office and what she showed me overnight in my dreams. Sharon said that another family member would like to speak with me too and she asked if I would talk with some police officers about the information I had picked up.

The following week two other members of Kiesha's family came to visit me. Steven and Sarah (not their real names) wanted to see if I could give them any more information about the little girl's whereabouts. At the time, I did not know how the family members were related to Kiesha's parents.

Steven had known Robert for many years. I asked him if anybody did any bike riding or BMX riding. Steven confirmed that, as children, he and Robert would ride motorbikes together. I told him about the images I had of bush tracks near electricity towers and Steven said that the area sounded very familiar. I mentioned a hotel where I felt that Robert drank — the name 'Plumpton Hotel' had immediately popped into my head. Steven confirmed that Robert had frequented the pub in the past. I was given the image of a delivery truck with the word 'Chippies' on the side and Steven said that Robert had worked for the company driving a delivery truck.

I was shown the image of a sports-type duffle bag that was round on both ends and had a carry strap. Steven said that he and Robert had owned bags like that for their motocross gear. I described the bag as quite large and again he agreed. I felt the bag was large enough to conceal Kiesha's body and Steven said, yes, it would be.

We talked about other visions I saw about Robert's life and the fact that Steven and Robert had become distant over the years. Steven was sickened to think that the friend he'd had since childhood could have been involved in Keisha's disappearance. Steven was a family man himself and the pride with which he spoke of his children was quite evident during our conversation. The most wonderful part of our reading was the fact that I could see that Steven and Sarah loved Kiesha and they were worried about her whereabouts. It was good to see that people actually cared about this tiny little fragile girl.

They asked me if I would be interested in speaking with a detective they called 'Detective Matt'. I never work on a missing person's or murder case unless asked to by a police officer working on the case. So I was not sure about getting involved in Kiesha's case until officially being asked.

◎　◎　◎

A short time later I received a phone call from Roger Mayer from the NSWPF Dog Unit. He asked if I was picking up anything to do with the case and if I was, if I would pass on to him any psychic information that I had picked up. Roger and his colleague Dave Cole were both working on Kiesha's case and I told them about the information I had received through holding her hat.

Roger was booked in to do a search with his dog Jeff and he asked if I would be interested in coming with him. I said that I was more than willing to go up to assist. I explained that over the previous few weeks I had Kiesha's spirit with me constantly. Since making the connection to her, she seemed to be quite connected to me.

Roger needed to get permission from the officer in charge of the case for me to accompany him. Because there was an urgency to have the Abrahams' property searched, Roger did a search with Jeff before the permission was granted. Dave Cole was also booked in to do a search with his dog Oscar. So it was suggested that I go to Mount Druitt with Dave and do a search for Kiesha. Again, we had to wait for permission for me to accompany him from the head of the taskforce.

I told Dave that I felt that Kiesha's parents were the perpetrators and that the little girl was deceased. I told him that I felt that Kiesha's body may have been placed in a sports duffle bag or suitcase. I passed on other relevant information from my visions, including about the bike trail and power lines, and I described the type of vegetation and area that I felt was connected to the case.

I could see bike riders passing by the area and that there were mounds of dirt that had been positioned to make jumps and ramps. Kiesha constantly showed me the image of someone riding a bike, and I just couldn't get it out of my head. It seemed very important for her to show me this image. I could smell fire and wondered if something had been burned or whether there had been a bushfire in the area. I felt that Kiesha's grave site was either in water or close to water, as I could smell muddy water and dampness when I tuned in to her.

I received further visions of where Kiesha was and I realised that she was buried and not in water because she showed me images of being under dirt and debris. Once again I could smell fire. I wondered if Kiesha was set on fire or was the smell connected to Kiesha in some other way?

I looked at maps online to get a better sense of the locations I was drawn to so that I could give the co-ordinates to Roger and Dave for their searches. I was looking for trail bike tracks, power lines, water and bush. Initially I was drawn to an area near the Sydney Olympic Regatta Centre at Castlereagh. Through Google images I could see that there were bike tracks along the waterways, but when I tuned in further something just didn't fit. On further investigation I dismissed this area.

Roger did do a search at the Abrahams' property. He said that Jeff did react in the garage area and he felt very strongly that Kiesha's remains had been present in that location. He confirmed that the area was full of rubbish and rolled-up carpet, which told me that I was on the right track. Roger noticed that there was an expensive lock on the garage door, but there wasn't anything of value inside. He said that this made him suspicious that the family had tried to hide something in the garage.

I rang Detective Matt and passed on the information that I had picked up concerning Kiesha's case. I also spoke to the detective inspector heading the case about what I had picked up while holding the hat. A few days later a reporter from a Sydney newspaper rang me about what I knew about the case.

The reporter was quite aware of the work I had been doing about Keisha, which was a surprise to me. She told me that she had been given permission by the police to write a story about the work I was doing on the case. I said that I didn't want to be involved and that I was not at all interested in being interviewed. I spoke to the detective inspector about the phone call and said that I wasn't going to do any interviews. He was happy with my decision. Unfortunately, it seems that the reporter had other ideas. I still don't know who leaked the information to her.

On the Friday of that week, Dave and I were planning to do a search with his dog Oscar around the Abrahams' property and in some bushland areas that I had pinpointed, but we were still waiting for approval. Then we were told that it would be postponed and would probably happen the following week.

◎　　◎　　◎

When the search was postponed, Roger Mayer and Dave Cole invited me to the NSW Police Dog Unit at Menai to watch the dog accreditation day. When I arrived around 11 am, I was quite nervous about how I would be received by the other officers, but my fears were laid to rest when I was introduced to other members of the squad — they were warm and very open to me.

Watching the dogs go through accreditation for their various tasks was incredible. I saw how the dogs are trained to detect drugs, bombs and cadavers. Firstly, the dogs were tested to see if they could detect any drugs in their training area. The officers showed me a cotton ball that had been impregnated with the smell of an illegal drug and hidden in a besser block wall. If a human smelt the cotton ball they would not detect the slightest fragrance at all. Yet these amazing police dogs could pinpoint the exact spot the cotton ball was placed within minutes.

Then the dogs were tested to detect bombs and gunpowder residue. Again, cotton balls impregnated with certain chemicals were placed in various locations. Each dog was run through around the location and they all went straight to the cotton balls.

Witnessing the teamwork between the officers and their dogs was fascinating. When the dogs had finished their work, their handlers would take them off to play as their reward. To see the two different sides of these incredible dogs was amazing. When they are working, they are extremely serious and focused — they are a force to be reckoned with and you would not want to get in their way. However, when they have finished the task, they are just like family dogs — they are playful, affectionate and very cheeky. The excitement on the dogs' faces when they are rewarded is priceless.

After the dogs finished their accreditation, I accompanied Roger and Dave with Oscar and Jeff to do some cadaver dog training. We went to an area a few kilometres away from the Dog Unit which had quite sparse bush, with red earth and gravel. Roger's dog Jeff was chosen to do the search, while Dave planted cotton balls impregnated with the scent of a cadaver. When planting the scents, Dave drove and leaned out of the car to place them. He did this so that his own scent wasn't left and the site was as uncontaminated as possible. Once Roger and Jeff began their search, there was no stopping them. Jeff is a very active and focused police dog and he located the cotton ball scents faster than it took Dave to lay them.

◎　◎　◎

The following morning I received a phone call from Dave, asking when I had conducted a search with police for Kiesha. I was totally shocked. I didn't know what he was talking about. As I don't get the daily newspapers, I wasn't aware that the reporter had run a story about me working with the police.

I was absolutely furious. To start with, I had told her that I was not interested in doing a story and I had told the detective inspector that I wouldn't do any interviews. Furthermore, I had not gone on any search. I was still waiting to get clearance to accompany Dave Cole or Roger Mayer to the sites. On the day that, according to the newspaper, I was supposed to be with police conducting a search, I was actually at the NSW Police Dog Unit at Menai with Roger and Dave.

This is the false story:

Psychic Tip on Kiesha Leads to Water

On the muddy bank of a western Sydney dam, homicide detectives watch the water drain, their hopes rising as the level falls.

Four months into their search for missing child Kiesha Abrahams, they are joined at the scene by uniformed police and specialist divers.

Not at the potential crime scene itself but not too far away at her home, clutching a piece of Kiesha's clothing, was the woman who had led them there — high-profile Sydney psychic Debbie Malone.

With every clue and lead run cold, homicide investigators took the extraordinary step of enlisting Ms Malone's help to find the girl's body.

'I didn't go to the police. They came to me,' Ms Malone said.

At Ms Malone's insistence, a dam near Penrith she believed may have been the dumping ground for the six-year-old's body was drained this week.

Kiesha was reported missing from her family's home in Woodstock Ave, Mt Druitt, on August 1.

Her mother Kristi Abrahams and stepfather Robert Smith have denied any involvement in her disappearance.

For almost 20 years Ms Malone has worked with police on unsolved murders in NSW and interstate. She lists the Belanglo backpacker murders, the disappearance of Sydney model Revelle Balmain and the murder of Southern Highlands mother Maria Scott among her high-profile cases.

Now, Ms Malone, a mother herself, has turned her hand to finding the curly brown-haired girl whose mysterious disappearance has troubled the hearts of thousands.

Ms Malone knows some officers scoff at her information and dismiss it.

But whatever she told detectives about Kiesha was credible enough for them to send a team to the dam near Penrith and drain it. It was not the first time police

Right: **Jeff, police cadaver dog.** Source: Roger Mayer

Middle: **Jeff searching for Kiesha in bushland.** Source: Roger Mayer

Below: **Officer Roger Mayer and his dog Jeff searching for Kiesha Abrahams in Sydney's western suburbs.** Source: Roger Mayer

have taken their search for Kiesha into the water, having waded through dams and creeks near her home in the days after she disappeared. But this time was different.

A senior police source would not talk specifically about what Ms Malone had told police, but confirmed she directed them to the dam: 'All I will say is it made sense to look there.'

It can also be revealed that a relative of Kiesha's mother and stepfather is assisting police with background information — and also working with Ms Malone.

'I am in contact with her [Kiesha's] family. They give me information to work with as well,' Ms Malone said.

But, as the bottom of the dam became clearer, hopes were dashed. Among the mud was debris and rubbish but not what Ms Malone and the police had expected to find there.

But they have not given up hope. Ms Malone said she had nominated some other dams to search.

I was not present with the police or the police divers and I did not give the police locations of other dams to be searched because I was never there. I had identified areas that I was going to visit with either Roger or Dave but this opportunity never arose. I had told the detective inspector that I needed to visit the area in person to ascertain if the area fitted my visions.

If something is written in the media, then people believe it. The fact that it was pure and utter lies is a gross injustice to me personally and the work I do with the police. I felt absolutely gutted by her lies. I felt as if I was a sacrificial lamb thrown to the wolves. To this day the reporter has never contacted me or apologised. Her vicious lies tarnished my name and the work I do with police. Not to mention it gave people the impression that I wasted the time of the police and their resources.

The picture of me accompanying the story was a file photograph taken the previous year in winter at St John's Park for another case I worked on with police. The search written about in the story supposedly took place on 3 December 2010, which was an extremely warm day. In the photograph I am wearing a brown jacket with a collared blouse underneath. My message to the reporter is: if you are going to write a story concerning a police case, always only write the whole truth and nothing but the truth — because the truth always comes out in the end and your lies will come back to haunt you.

When the story was published, I really questioned why I do the work I do. I don't charge to work on police cases and I do so much pro bono work with families. I wondered if continuing to do this type of work was worth all the stress and anguish I put myself through. I spoke with Dave and Roger and, after a lot of soul-searching , decided that I wasn't going to let this journalist stop me from helping officers who ask for my assistance.

On a very positive note I have had the privilege of working with amazing police officers in different states of Australia. I am very privileged to have been able to work with amazing officers like Roger Mayer and Dave Cole. Through my work I feel that I have made some amazing connections and friendships that I truly treasure.

*   *   *

After Kiesha's disappearance, Kristi Abrahams and Robert Smith moved out of their apartment and into a motel. They told police they had done so because of the ongoing media attention. Once their unit was empty, the police methodically searched it for any vital clues that could help with their investigation. Investigating officers seized Kiesha's mattress, bedding and carpet for testing. The laboratory reports picked up traces of Kiesha's blood throughout the unit. On the wooden frame of Kiesha's bed, teeth marks were found.

A few days later the couple returned to the apartment. The police had installed a recording device during the search and were listening. The first thing they heard Kristi say was, 'They've taken her mattress — they'll only find her piss and shit on it.' For a mother who was supposedly mourning her missing child, these were cold and heartless words.

The couple subsequently moved to another government-subsidised house, which had also been bugged by the police. If you were looking for your missing child and you thought she had been abducted, why would you move away from the home where she lived before you knew what had happened to her? This is not the action of a loving family missing their little girl.

In December 2010, police used undercover officers to befriend the couple and to try to gain the couple's confidence. Robert Smith came to regard them as 'friends' and began to drop his guard. On the night of 21 April 2011, unaware that they were being monitored and recorded, Kristi and Robert met the two undercover officers at a hotel in Sydney and they disclosed information about Kiesha that was crucial to the case.

Kristi Abrahams said that approximately two weeks before she was reported missing, Kiesha had been in her bedroom crying when Kristi wanted her to put on her pyjamas. When the little girl resisted, her mother gave her a 'little nudge' with her foot. Kristi said that Kiesha jumped and hit her head on the bottom of her bed and went 'funny'. Kristi put Kiesha under the shower in an attempt to wake her up and said that she felt like 'jelly'. Instead of calling an ambulance, Kristi and Robert Smith put Kiesha on a foldout bed and then went off to sleep. In the morning when they awoke, Kiesha was no longer breathing.

The couple told the officers that Robert took a suitcase from their garage, put the tiny body inside and left it in the wardrobe in Kiesha's bedroom for several days. I feel that the couple moved the suitcase to the garage and left her body there until they disposed of it.

Robert Smith then rode his pushbike around the local area to try and find a suitable burial site in bushland where they could dispose of Kiesha's body. After locating a site, the couple called a taxi at around 5 am on Sunday, 18 July 2010 using a false name and address. They took the taxi to the remote site that Robert had chosen. (When I learned this, I understood why it was so important for Kiesha to keep showing me the image of a person riding a bike. She was trying to show me what her stepfather had done to her.) He made a shallow hole using a hammer and tipped Kiesha's body out of the suitcase into the hole. Then he poured petrol over the body and he set it alight.

This gave the undercover agents enough information to arrest the couple. However, before they could arrest them, they needed to find out where Kiesha's body had been buried so that she could be laid to rest. Fortunately, Kristi and Robert were eager to prove to them that they were telling them the truth about what happened to Kiesha. That night they agreed to take the officers with them to the burial site.

The next night, on the 22 April, which would have been Kiesha's seventh birthday, Kristi and Robert led the undercover agents to the shallow grave in Freya Crescent at Shalvey. When they left the lonely bush grave where they had dumped Kiesha's body, they were met by Detectives Russell Oxford and Andrew Marks. They were arrested and taken to Mount Druitt Police Station, where they were formally charged with the child's murder.

Forensic investigators examined Kiesha's skeletal remains and found teeth and fragments of her hair in the dirt. Her teeth were chipped and fractured, injuries that were found to have occurred near to or at the time of her death. The postmortem conducted by Dr Orde revealed that Kiesha suffered 'significant and considerable damage' to her head, face and shoulders. The injuries that Kiesha endured were severe. Dr Orde stated that if Kiesha was conscious when the physical abuse took place, she would have suffered significantly. There was also evidence of bone injuries that dated from the final weeks or months before her murder.

The court found that Kiesha had suffered years of physical abuse at the hands of her mother. Kristi Abrahams was found guilty of murder and interfering with a corpse, and was sentenced to 22 years and six months, with a minimum non-parole period of 16 years. Kiesha's stepfather Robert Smith was charged with manslaughter on the grounds of 'gross criminal negligence' and was sentenced to a maximum of 16 years in gaol with a 12-year non-parole period.

◎   ◎   ◎

On the morning of 21 November 2012, Kiesha's birth father Chris Weippeart was found dead in his bed. Police sources said that Chris suffered from type 1 diabetes and was a known drug user. It is thought that Chris passed away from natural causes due to his health issues.

Chris Weippeart was also the birth father of Kiesha's older brother Ayden, who was born on 6 February 2003 and was found dead six weeks later. It is believed that he died from sudden infant death syndrome (SIDS) — the postmortem found the cause of death to be 'unascertained'.

◎   ◎   ◎

CONFIRMATION OF PSYCHIC VISIONS

After Kiesha's body was found, many of the psychic visions I had seen were confirmed. I did not find her remains, however Kiesha did share a lot of information with me pertaining to her case.

- Kiesha was found to have head injuries and her teeth were broken due to her mother assaulting her.
- Kiesha had been subjected to prolonged physical abuse in the months prior to her death.

- There was evidence that Kristi had burned Kiesha on the face with a cigarette when she was aged three. She also had a black eye from her mother hitting her.
- Kiesha's body was kept in the house in a suitcase for over a week before being disposed of. (I still believe that her remains were kept in the garage. When Roger Mayer and his cadaver dog Jeff searched the area, Jeff had a positive reaction in the garage.)
- Robert Smith rode around the local area on his bicycle to find a suitable place to dump Keisha's body.
- The body was put into a suitcase and dumped in a bushland area surrounded by eucalyptus trees.
- Kiesha's body was found in a place that was close to water and from where power lines were visible.
- There were bike tracks leading through the area and close to where Kiesha's remains were found.
- Robert had buried Kiesha in a shallow grave, which is why I could see and smell dirt.
- He poured petrol onto Kiesha's remains and set fire to them. This is why I kept picking up the smell of something burning, which I thought could have been a bushfire.
- I could see from my visions that Kiesha's mother and stepfather were the murderers.

◉ ◉ ◉

This case was very difficult to work on. As a mother it was hard to even comprehend how another mother could mistreat her own child in the way that Kristi did.

On a personal level, this case was truly a struggle, and it made me question my work right to the very core of my being. Seeing what little Kiesha went through was challenging and haunting. The challenges with the press was another reason I questioned my work. The positive to this case that even though a beautiful little angel was taken from this life so early, justice was done.

Every time I see a butterfly or see the colour purple I remember what a brave and courageous little angel Kiesha was. I take these signs as a message that she is now safe and well in the spirit world. The signs also confirm to me that I should continue doing what I do. I hope that Keisha knows and understands how many lives she touched in the small time that she was on this earth.

Chapter 2

The Murders at Murphy's Creek

In 2004, I worked on the television program *Sensing Murder*. The episode on the Murphy's Creek case, called 'A Mother's Instinct' which aired in 2005, was one of four I worked on for the Australian program.

The psychics on the program were not given any information about the cases — which were all cold cases — and we were all kept apart and filmed separately. Four of the cases I worked on were interstate and one was in New Zealand and I had no prior knowledge about any of them — at the time the Murphy's Creek murders took place I was 11 years of age.

The *Sensing Murder* episodes were always shot over a two-day period, the first day in a studio. I had approximately one hour in the studio to work on the case and pick up as much information as possible before being interviewed. Then it was time to leave the studio and no further comment was allowed about the case — I was not allowed to discuss it with any of the crew — and any other psychic who was working on the case was filmed on a different day and was kept entirely apart from me (I didn't meet Deb Webber, the other psychic on the Murphy's Creek episode until 2011).

◎   ◎   ◎

Lorraine Wilson, aged 20, and Wendy Evans, 18, were nurses who worked at St George Hospital in Sydney. They were holidaying in Queensland in September and October 1974. Lorraine's VW Beetle broke down near Goondiwindi, a town near the New South Wales border. While the car was in for repair, they decided to hitch-hike the 350 kilometres northeast to Brisbane to visit Wendy's sister. They stayed with her for a few days and then set off to hitch back to Goondiwindi to pick up the car. This was the last time Wendy's sister saw the young women alive.

The two women were reported missing on 12 October 1974. Their skeletal remains were found on Friday, 25 June

Lorraine Wilson (left) **and Wendy Evans.** Source: Eric Wilson

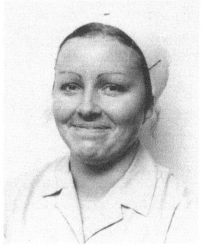

Lorraine Wilson as a nursing
trainee. Source: Eric Wilson

Trainee nurse Wendy Evans.
Source: Eric Wilson

1976 by two bush walkers who were walking in bushland near Murphy's Creek, Toowoomba.

In November 1985, a coronial inquest was held into the deaths of Wendy Joy Evans and Lorraine Ruth Wilson. The coroner found that the two women had been murdered by a person or persons unknown, between 6 October and 12 October 1974.

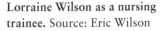

The Murphy's Creek murders is one of the most horrific cases I have ever worked on. I will never forget being a psychic witness to the cruelty and barbarism the perpetrators inflicted on two innocent young women.

I was flown to Brisbane, checked into a hotel and then went straight to the studio. When I do a reading I usually tune in via psychometry, which involves holding a piece of jewellery or other personal possession. I was given a gold ring, which had a moon and star design with a tiny little pearl in the middle. Initially, when I observed the ring and its design I was put off by its age and the feelings I picked up from it. I knew that there was a history to this ring and I felt that it had had more than one owner. I tried to tune in to the victim, and not all of the previous owners, so that I could pick up her story. I sat with the ring for about five minutes and then began to explain on camera that I could see two females who I felt were the victims in the case.

When I held the ring I could feel the strong presence of a young woman. She suddenly appeared in my mind's eye. She had long, light brown straight hair and beautiful brown eyes, a big white smile and she told me that she was as tall as I am — 168 centimetres (5 feet 5 inches). I could see by her hairstyle and the way she was dressed that the crime had happened some time back. Her clothing looked like it came from the 1970s — she was wearing flared denim jeans, a T-shirt and platform shoes.

A second woman stood before me. She was shorter and of a more solid build. This young woman had shoulder-length, wavy brown hair and a very cheeky smile with dimples in her cheeks. I felt that she was slightly younger than the other victim and that these two women were inseparable.

The first woman, who I later discovered was Lorraine Wilson, communicated with me the most. Lorraine began to reveal that something had happened to her car. I could see that the young women had their bags packed and I felt that they had gone on a holiday — when I see the image of bags or suitcases, it means a holiday or that the person is moving. In this case, the trip was supposed to be the holiday of a lifetime. I could see that they came from Sydney and had travelled up to Queensland. A map of New South Wales and Queensland began to form in my mind.

The image of a map of Brisbane became very clear. I was told by Lorraine that I needed to drive northwest of Brisbane to find the location where the girls were murdered.

I felt that the ring had a significant family connection. Lorraine then showed me a link to her mother and grandmother. Later I was told that the ring had been handed down through the family, from Lorraine's grandmother to her mother Betty, then to Lorraine. After Lorraine's death, it was passed to her niece who unfortunately she never met. I was also given two black-and-white photographs of the victims to hold. The first was of Lorraine dressed in her nurse's uniform with a stethoscope around her neck. The second photograph was a side-on shot of Wendy dressed in what looks like a formal outfit with her hair pulled up into a bun.

As soon as I held Lorraine's photograph I knew that she was the one who owned the ring I had been holding. The initial image I had of her in my mind's eye was the exact image I was now seeing in the photograph. The photograph of the other woman also fitted my psychic vision. Wendy came across to me as a much quieter and shyer person who preferred to stay in the background. I could see her standing beside Lorraine. However Wendy let Lorraine communicate with me to explain what had happened to them both.

WHAT I SAW PSYCHICALLY

Much of what I saw was confirmed in evidence that came to light during the second coronial inquest and through the *60 Minutes* episode called 'Murder at Murphy's Creek'.

The Victims

VICTIM 1: Lorraine Ruth
   Wilson
AGE: Late teens to early 20s
HEIGHT: Approximately
   168 cm
BUILD: Tall, thin build
HAIR: Long, straight light
   brown hair
EYES: Large brown eyes

Source: Eric Wilson

DISTINGUISHING FEATURES:
   Big white teeth when she smiled
PERSONALITY: Fun-loving, very sweet, caring, innocent,
   trusting, very close to her family, hard worker, full
   of life and adventurous.

VICTIM 2: Wendy Joy Evans
AGE: Late teens — around
   18 years of age
HEIGHT: Approximately
   155–158 cm
BUILD: Solid build, slightly
   overweight
HAIR: Shoulder-length
   wavy brown hair
EYES: Blue

Source: Eric Wilson

DISTINGUISHING FEATURES:
   Cheeky smile, dimples when she smiled
PERSONALITY: Fun-loving, very sweet, shy, caring,
   innocent, trusting, thoughtful, hard worker.

The Circumstances

- The young women were upset and wanted to be taken home.
- They were on a holiday.
- The car they were travelling in had broken down.
- They had hitch-hiked after the car broke down.
- Both women said to me that they were told by their mothers that they shouldn't hitch-hike.
- They told me that their family said they should catch a bus rather than hitch-hike.
- The young women were best friends and went everywhere together — they were like sisters.
- They were both students.
- I could see an image of hands. This image is an indication that the person is gentle and caring — it can also mean that the person may be a healer or works in the health sector.
- The young women both said goodbye to their families and were never seen again.
- They were given a lift; however, they never arrived at their final destination.
- The women knew one of the offenders.
- They were very innocent and trusting.
- The young women told me that they hitch-hiked from Brisbane. They showed me a map of Queensland and said that if you looked at a map you would go from the left of Brisbane and up to the hills, which is where their bodies were found in the Toowoomba Ranges.

The Vehicle/s

Vehicle 1

- I was shown an older car — a Holden — that was two tone (green and light green) with a white roof and venetian blinds in the back window. I heard the words 'EH Holden'.
- The interior was beige or light coloured.
- The car had square tail-lights.

Key differences between EJs and EHs

During the inquest there was confusion about whether the vehicle the women were picked up by was an EJ or EH Holden. These cars are very similar in appearance. The three most obvious differences between an EJ and EH sedan are:

- The tail-lights – the EJ has oval tail-lights and a more rounded back; the EH has more rectangular tail-lights and a squared back.
- Cowl vents under the windscreen: – the EJ sedan has two separate vents with chrome surrounds the EH has a single, long vent.
- The fuel cap – the cap on the EJ is hinged; the EH has a round cap.

EH Holden

Vehicle 2

- This vehicle joined the first car at the murder scene. It was a dark-coloured, square-shaped sedan, similar to a Ford Falcon sedan — possibly a 1965 XP model. The tail-lights were round.

Vehicle 3

- I saw a red ute that looked like an old Ford F100 ute, with a dog in the back. The dog looked like a cattle/hunting dog. The vehicle had a white steering wheel and a red metal dashboard. I was not sure if the interior was also red.
- I saw the ute at a rural property and then parked at a swimming area near a river or water hole.
- I did not see the third vehicle at the murder scene — however it could have joined the perpetrators at a later stage of the night during the rapes and subsequent murders.
- I know that there is a definite connection between the red ute and one of the perpetrators because the image was so clear. I saw the vehicle in multiple visions, which confirms to me that the vehicle is of some importance to the case.

The Location/s

Queensland

- The young women showed me a map of Queensland.
- I could see that they were taken to a party — the words were 'house party'.

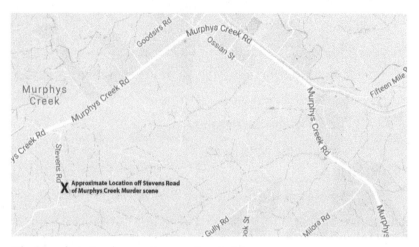

The Murphy's Creek area. Source: Google Maps

- The women were later taken to a rural location near a riverbed where they were sexually assaulted and murdered.
- The riverbed may have dried up since.
- There was gravel or sandy soil at the location as I could hear crunching underfoot.
- Campfire — the men had been to the location before drinking beer and yahooing. I could also see that the men had taken other female victims to the campfire previously. I question if other attacks on females had taken place at the same location prior to Lorraine and Wendy's deaths? Had these attacks happened and not been reported to police?

Date of the Crime

- The type of clothing and shoes worn by the victims indicated that the crime took place in the early to mid 1970s.

The Perpetrators

- The perpetrators were male.
- There were two main perpetrators, who were joined by others at the murder scene.
- I picked up the feeling that some of the perpetrators could now be dead.
- Some of the perpetrators may have gone to gaol for sexual offences unrelated to the women's murders.
- I felt the perpetrators were local and were familiar with the murder site — I could see that they had been to the murder site previously.
- The men had committed other attacks in the same area prior to the murders.
- I felt the perpetrators worked at an abattoir, butchery or similar.
- The perpetrators were cruel and had possibly committed cruelty to animals.
- The perpetrators were known to police and possibly had criminal records.
- They were known for their violence and they had extremely bad tempers.
- They were part of a gang or group that inflicted violence on women.
- Some of the men could be married and had inflicted violence on their wives or partners.
- The men were known to frequent the local pubs and were not good with alcohol.
- People in the town knew the men and were frightened of them — they were a law unto themselves.

- I could see that the two main perpetrators had tattoos. One was of a snake on a man's forearm — it looked like it was on the right forearm — and the snake was coiled up and possibly wrapped around something like a dagger. I can't definitely say which of the two main perpetrators the tattoo belonged to because I could only see the forearm of the man as he attacked the victims. During the 1970s tattoos were not as popular as they are today, so this would have been noticeable. It was believed that those with tattoos came from lower socioeconomic backgrounds and that tattoos were statements about the wearer's status in society. Tattoos were worn as a badge of honour, sometimes delineating gang membership, showing the wearer was tough. The feeling I got was that the men felt proud of their tattoos as they were a statement as to who they were and their place in society.

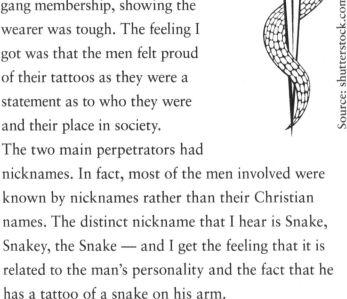

Source: shutterstock.com

- The two main perpetrators had nicknames. In fact, most of the men involved were known by nicknames rather than their Christian names. The distinct nickname that I hear is Snake, Snakey, the Snake — and I get the feeling that it is related to the man's personality and the fact that he has a tattoo of a snake on his arm.

Perpetrator 1

HEIGHT: 180-182 cm

HAIR: Long wavy brown hair parted to the side.

EYES: Blue eyes, ice cold when challenged.

BUILD: Tall, thin build.

APPEARANCE: He was well groomed, clean shaven, with chiselled features and a nice smile. Possibly had a broken nose and scars to the face from physical conflicts or fights.

AGE: 20s to early 30s.

DISTINGUISHING FEATURES: Tattoos upper and lower arms, calloused hands.

CLOTHING: Jeans and a light-coloured shirt with the sleeves rolled up.

PERSONALITY: Cold, controlling, bad tempered, cruel, violent. A habitual reoffender, he was known for physical assaults, sexual attacks and rapes of women, as well as cruelty to animals. He liked to pick fights, and was known to be a thug and stand-over man. He had attacked and raped women before the murders and may have committed crimes afterwards. Smoker. Known by a nickname.

VOCATION: Trade type work, possibly at an abattoir.

HOME: Lived in a rural area.

Perpetrator 2

HEIGHT: Approximately 170 cm

HAIR: Brown

EYES: Possibly dark coloured – hazel green–brown – beady, squinty

BUILD: Stocky

APPEARANCE: Scruffy, untidy, muscular arms

AGE: 20s to early 30s

DISTINGUISHING FEATURES: Tattoos, upper arm and possibly lower forearms

CLOTHING: Jeans and button-up collared shirt

PERSONALITY: Serial rapist, known for violence against women, enjoyed inflicting pain, big drinker, picked fights (often when intoxicated). Smoker. Control freak and mentally unstable. Also known by a nickname. Cruel to animals.

VOCATION: Trade-type work, possibly at an abattoir. May have worked with Perpetrator 1.

Weapons

- I was shown a weapon that was kept under the front seat of the car — it looked like a tyre lever or wheel brace.
- Baseball bat.
- Rope with which the young women were tied up — thin white cord, similar to the type used on venetian blinds.

Injuries/Cause of Death

- I saw Lorraine being dragged by her long hair.
- Sexual assault — the words I was given were 'gang bang'.
- I had the feeling that some men joined the group at the time of the attack. They came in separate vehicles.

- I could see that the nurses were hog-tied — bound by the feet and hands as if they were animals.
- I could see that the women had been gagged to stop them from speaking or screaming.
- They were bludgeoned to death and suffered severe head injuries and trauma to the body.
- I could see one man stomping on and kicking one of the women as she lay on the ground. One of the women suffered severe injuries to the back left side of the head.
- The other had severe head injuries to the face and to the side of the head.
- I could see that they were repeatedly hit about the head — one woman's face was completely beaten to a pulp. The pain I experienced while tuning in during this vision was absolutely horrendous.

Other Significant Information

- A red-headed woman was aware of what happened to the nurses, but she never came forward to police about the crimes.
- I had a very strong feeling that another woman was aware of the events that took place on the day of the murder — I even wondered whether she was at the murder scene during the time of the crime.
- I heard the words 'Old Quarry'. The area had big sandstone-coloured rocks. (Later I discovered that there is an old quarry near Murphy's Creek in the Helidon area that was used as a swimming hole and

that some of the men were known to visit at the time
of the murders.)

- The swimming hole was known to locals and I felt
  the men had taken other women there in the past.
  Although I do not see the nurses at this location, it
  has some connection to the perpetrators.

- I saw the nurses being taken to a home with a number
  of vehicles parked at the front, including the red ute
  and the green-and-white EH sedan (vehicles 1 and 3).
  I watched as the women were taken inside the house
  and introduced to an older woman with red hair.

- The house looked like it was situated on an elevated
  block with a verandah at the front. It had a view of
  paddocks or rural land in the distance. The property
  looked a bit run down, with old farm machinery and
  disused equipment and abandoned vehicles close to
  the front of the house.

- The feeling I received from the young women was
  that of excitement about going to a social event such
  as a BBQ or party. There were a number of men at
  the location.

- There was an older woman at the home who felt as
  if she was the mother of one or more of the people at
  the property. There was a young boy at the location,
  who I could see in the kitchen area with the older
  woman.

- I could see the two nurses speaking with the older
  woman in the house and I got the feeling that they
  felt safe and secure because there was another
  woman there.

- I was shown the number 6 — the girls were murdered on 6 October and their bodies were found in the sixth month of the year, in June 1976.
- I was shown a birthday cake and felt great sadness because I didn't make this celebration. Lorraine was 20 at the time of her murder and she had been very excited about her upcoming 21st birthday.
- The murder scene has been frequently visited by the men in the past.
- I heard screaming and yelling, which went on for hours.
- The young women told me persistently that people knew what happened to them and nobody did anything to help them.
- More males joined the two main perpetrators at the time of the rape, attack and murder of the two girls.
- There was no attempt to cover up the crime. Lorraine's and Wendy's battered bodies were left were they were bludgeoned to death in open bush.
- I saw platform shoes with cork heels, clothing and a distinct denim handbag.
- Belongings were scattered everywhere.
- There were remains of a campfire, burned wooden logs, beer cans and beer bottles.
- I could see that one or more of the perpetrators had taken a trophy belonging to one or both of the victims as a memento of what they had done (Lorraine's ring). I feel that they may have tried to sell the item to make a personal financial gain.

- The perpetrators returned to the murder scene to gloat over their escapades.
- Animals had gone through the murder site, as I could see that the bones were bleached white due to being exposed to the elements, and they had been scattered around the murder scene.
- I could see someone using a metal detector at the murder scene to locate lost items and jewellery.
- The ring I was given to tune in to also had the energy of another person in it. I felt that it had belonged to a grandmother as well as the victim, who I felt was Lorraine, and I also saw a woman younger than Lorraine wearing it.

◎　◎　◎

On the second day of filming I was taken out to Murphy's Creek. The car stopped on the side of a road that led up a hill. The area was quite bushy and isolated. There weren't any houses in sight.

I was asked if I could find the site where the nurses were murdered. Instantly, the victims Lorraine and Wendy guided me to cross the road, walk into long grass and then through scrub. I had to climb over a barbed-wire fence and was guided to keep walking deeper and deeper into the bush. Then I was led into a clearing where I could see some logs placed in the centre as though being used as seats, and there were the remnants of a campfire. Littered throughout the area were discarded beer cans, some of which were very old steel cans which were not manufactured after the

1980s. The most prominent brand was XXXX made by Castlemaine.

The location felt as if it held secrets and memories. It was a place where men would gather around the campfire and drink until they passed out. When I stood near the fire site I was taken back in time — I could hear men talking, telling stories and bragging about their sexual exploits. I felt that those men who visited this place did so regularly. The area was quite ordinary — it wasn't picturesque — and it wasn't somewhere you would go to unless there was a purpose.

The day was quite warm and the place was deathly still without the slightest breath of air. I was alarmed by the feeling of eeriness I got at the campfire. It was not somewhere you would like to visit alone, especially if you were female. The isolation was something I will never forget — if you were in any danger and you screamed for help, nobody would hear

The crime scene at Murphy's Creek. Source: Queensland Police Service

you. I could sense fear and dread begin to engulf me. The fear that seemed to emanate from the bush was something I will never forget.

When I walked to an area in the clearing not far from the campfire, I felt an overwhelming feeling of dread. Sap dripping from a tree in front of me looked like blood dripping from a person. I felt that this was a sign of the bloodshed that had taken place there.

◎　◎　◎

Over a decade has passed since I worked on the *Sensing Murder* episode. This case — and the horrific way the women were murdered — has always haunted me. What has haunted me most is that no-one was brought to justice for these horrendous crimes.

After the airing of the episode, I hoped that somebody would come forward with new information about the murders. The evidence that came to light at that point was supplemented by a large amount of information presented at a second inquest, which was held in 2013. The following year Michael Usher did a story on the case for *60 Minutes* (see below). With the continuing interest in the murders, new witnesses have come forward and now many of the missing pieces of the murder jigsaw puzzle have been put into place. This new information has confirmed many of the visions I saw during my time working on the Murphy's Creek murders, particularly the evidence from the coroner's findings of 2013.

SENSING MURDERS SCREENING, 2005

Vivian and Rose Murphy contacted the police after the episode was shown. The program had reminded the couple of an incident they had witnessed, although they could not give precise details about when it had occurred. In 1974 the Murphys lived in Dalby in the Darling Downs, which is about 200 kilometres northwest of Brisbane, and the family frequently travelled to the north Brisbane suburb of Redcliffe to visit Mrs Murphy's mother.

The Murphys said that as they were driving along the Toowoomba Range Road with their children, a young woman came running out onto the road. Mrs Murphy said that the woman was being pursued by a man, whom she described as being of average build and height with dark hair. As they slowly passed by, the young woman reached out her hands and cried out, 'Help! Help! Help!' Mrs Murphy said there was another couple on the left-hand side of the road near a parked car. The Murphys said they were too frightened to stop but they went to the Helidon police station and reported the incident. The police did not follow up on the incident report at the time.

THE SECOND CORONIAL INQUEST, 2013

The coroner interviewed many witnesses during the inquest and these are his findings.

Persons of interest

At the time the nurses were murdered, a group of men reined terror over the locals of Toowoomba. These men came primarily from two extended and interrelated family groups: the Hiltons and the Lauries. They were known for their violence and their attacks on both males and females. It was reported that they liked nothing more than to give their victims a 'hiding'. Every Friday, Saturday and Sunday night, the men would meet at the local pub and drink excessively, and afterwards drive around the Toowoomba area and pick up unsuspecting females. They would force the women into their cars and proceed to bash and rape them.

Former Homicide Squad Detective Inspector Kerry Johnson identified seven men as persons of interest in the murder case. Allan John 'Shortie' Laurie, Wayne 'Boogie' Hilton, Donald 'Donnie' Laurie and Larry Charles are deceased. At the time of writing, Allan Neil 'Ungie' Laurie, Terrence James 'Jimmy' O'Neill and Desmond 'Dessie' Roy Hilton were still alive.

Wayne 'Boogie' Hilton, who was identified as the man who forced Lorraine Wilson into a car, had confessed to his boss Neil Shum that he had killed the nurses. He was known to be a thug and a rapist. He was also known to carry items such as tyre levers and baseball bats in his car and use them to bash victims. At the time of the murders he was working at the Toowoomba bacon factory — the cord that was found at the murder scene was the same cord that was used at the factory to slice through offal. Boogie Hilton was known to wear a silver signet ring inset with a large coloured stone, which had gone missing around the time of the murder. A very similar ring was found at the murder scene — it was part of police evidence that was lost during the years of investigations.

The coroner found that Boogie Hilton committed the murders in the presence of others who could not be firmly identified. Hilton died in a car crash aged 31, in 1986 at Texas, Queensland, and was never charged with the murders.

The Charles family is related to both the Hilton and Laurie families. Larry Charles was riddled with guilt over the fate of the two women. He shot himself on 3 July 1985, the day after confessing his part in the murders to his friend, Desmond 'Dessie' Edmondstone. He said that he was present at the rapes and murders of the two women. Edmondstone claimed that Charles told him that he had skulled rum (which he never drank) to make himself pass out because he couldn't stand to hear the women's agonising screams.

Donald 'Donnie' Laurie, who died in 1993 at the age of 54, allegedly admitted that he was present on that night, but said he didn't kill the nurses. He said that the women were tied to a tree and he felt sorry for them and wanted to give them water. He told another witness that on the day after the murders he and Boogie Hilton had returned to the murder scene to move the women's bodies — when he got back, he was seen washing blood off his hands. He was terrified he would be arrested for the murders.

Allan 'Shortie' Laurie was celebrating his 22nd birthday on the day of the murders. He was an extremely violent man, who was known to have bashed his mother and stomped on her head, and had bitten off his father's ear in a fight over a sausage. He was known to be a serial rapist and for his extreme violence. When Shortie Laurie was interviewed by police about the women's murders, he went beserk and began to bellow like a bull. Police could not continue their interview and he was set free. He died in a car accident at the age of 48. Dessie Hilton, who admitted to cleaning blood out of a car the morning after the murders, identified Shortie Laurie as one of the men who told him to do so.

Another of the men who instructed Dessie Hilton to clean the car was Allan 'Ungie' Laurie, who was 25 years old at the time of the murders and had a reputation for violence. The second inquest heard that he was one of three men who had bragged that they had given a hiding to some nurses at the bottom of the range.

Trevor Hilton, who was related to Boogie Hilton, gave evidence to police on a number of occasions that he had seen Shortie Laurie, Ungie Laurie and Boogie Hilton assaulting women and pushing them into cars. He said that the three of them were known to carry tyre levers, wheel spanners and/or baseball bats in their cars to use as weapons. He said they openly bragged about forcing women into cars so that they could have sex with them.

Terrence 'Jimmy' O'Neill was 23 years old at the time of the murders. He was a friend of both the Laurie and Hilton families. Larry Charles told Dessie Edmondstone that Jimmy O'Neill was present at the rape of the two women. At the time O'Neill owned a green-and-white EH Holden, although he later denied it despite there being pictures of him with the car. He was quoted as saying, 'Getting a smack in the mouth is not violent.' No findings were made against him.

DISCOVERY OF THE VICTIMS' REMAINS

On Friday 25 June 1976, an elderly couple who were bushwalking parked their car on a dirt track near Murphy's Creek and walked through a gateway into a wooded area. About 100 metres from the fence line, at a clearing, they stumbled across the remains and personal items of the missing nurses. The couple went back to their car and set off for Toowoomba police station, but on the way came across a police car. They stopped and reported their discovery. Detectives from Brisbane were summoned immediately. A transistor radio found at the scene had Lorraine Wilson's named engraved on it, pointing to the identity of the victims.

THE CRIME SCENE

The vicinity in which the remains were found was searched thoroughly by the police helped by army personnel using metal detectors.

The remains were relatively intact, although some of the bones were found scattered in a 20 metre radius. There were decayed pieces of clothing belonging to the young women on both skeletons. They were still wearing jeans and underwear and their bra straps were still fastened. Both women had been hog-tied with cord tied around both ankles and linked together.

Police searching Murphy's Creek after the remains of Lorraine Wilson and Wendy Evans were discovered in 1976. Source: Queensland Police Service

The nurses' belongings were found close by. Some items were grouped together as if they had fallen from a bag or suitcase. The items included toothbrushes, hair brushes, cigarette lighters and jewellery (two rings and an astrological cancer sign pendant). Their bankbooks, chequebooks and wallets were not found at the crime scene.

Two rings were found at the murder scene. One was identified by Lorraine's mother as belonging to her daughter. It was the distinct gold ring I held and tuned in to Lorraine while working on *Sensing Murder*. The other ring — a white metal dress signet ring inset with a distinctive coloured stone — did not belong to either of the victims and was a type commonly worn by males at the time. Boogie Hilton was known to wear a similar ring, although his ring may have been gold, not silver or white gold. As stated earlier, this ring was held as evidence by police; however, it mysteriously disappeared at some point during the investigation.

RESULTS OF AUTOPSIES

Lorraine Wilson and Wendy Evans were both identified by their dental records. Lorraine's skull was relatively intact but showed major fractures to the left back of her head. It was estimated that one to three blows to the head would have caused her fatal injuries. Wendy had extensive injuries to her facial area and to the top and both sides of her head, resulting in severe fractures. She suffered multiple injuries, indicating that her face would have been 'bashed to a pulp'. She received many strikes to the head which were more than sufficient to have killed her.

WITNESSES

Due to the media attention generated by the second inquest, a number of women came forward and made statements about what they experienced at the hands of the Hilton and Laurie Gang. Three of them described violence and sexual assaults that they endured for extended periods by the members of the Laurie-Hilton gang. All three said that they had been raped by members of the gang on separate occasions. They all named Shortie Laurie as one of the men responsible for their attacks and rapes.

Some of the victims reported their sexual assaults to police. However, the officers at the time didn't fully investigate the women's claims. It is disappointing that their cases were not followed up. If investigated properly, the perpetrators may have been caught and the murders of Wendy Evans and Lorraine Wilson may never have taken place. It is very disappointing that the gang were allowed to roam the streets unanswerable to anyone for such a long period of time.

Rape victim 1: Anne alleges she was raped by two men, one she identified as Shortie Lawrence [sic], in 1974 when she was 19. She said that she was offered a lift home on a Saturday night. She recalled that the car she was picked up in was a light-coloured sedan but was unsure of the make and model. The two men took her to an open area behind Downlands College, parked the car and both men raped her. After the sexual assault, they dropped her off across the road from her home. Anne told her father what had happened and they reported the incident to police. She was given a medical examination and her clothes were taken. Anne didn't hear anything further from the police about the incident. She said she was too frightened to contact the police to ask about their investigation.

She later heard rumours that other young women had experienced similar sexual assaults.

Rape victim 2: Gail first met Shortie Laurie and his brothers Gordon and Ian in 1969 when she was 16 years old. She said that the men would offer to give young women lifts home but they would never take them straight home. Once they had the victims in their car, there was no chance of escape — Gail said that the men had removed the door handles and window winders so their victims could not get out. When she asked why there were no handles, the men said that the car was being repaired. They would take the girls to a bush paddock near Toowoomba and force alcohol on them to get them intoxicated to the point of being paralytic. The men took turns raping Gail. She said she was raped so many times that she lost count.

Rape victim 3: Kerry-Ann was 15 years old in 1974 and had run away from home when she was picked up by a man she knew as 'Shortie'. He was a truck driver in the Goondiwindi area at the time. He drove her to an isolated area and repeatedly raped her. Kerry-Ann said that after the initial assault, other men known to Shortie picked her up and raped her on many occasions. She said that a gang of men, comprising the Lauries, the Hiltons and associates, roamed the Goondiwindi and Toowoomba area cruising for prey.

Ian Hamilton: On the evening of 6 October 1974, Hamilton, then a police officer on duty at the Toowoomba traffic branch, was called to the Yukarnavale Youth Camp on the uphill section of Toowoomba Range Road. The caretakers reported that they could hear a woman screaming and it had been going on for around 30 minutes. Hamilton and his partner arrived at the camp just after 9 pm. Initially, he didn't hear anything, but after a few minutes he heard the screams too. He described them as 'the most terrifying and horrendous screams he had ever experienced — blood curdling'. The officers searched the area for 30 to 40 minutes but, because there was a blustery wind, they could not pinpoint the direction the screams were coming from. At around midnight they returned to the police station and notified the officers who were commencing their shift what had occurred.

This incident occurred a week before the two nurses were reported missing. Unfortunately, it was not investigated further until the women's remains were found two years later. Hamilton said at that point he checked his records, confirmed the date the incident took place and passed his information on to the Homicide Squad detectives investigating the case. He also passed on intelligence about a group of men who were known to be committing sexual assaults in the town of Toowoomba. The members of this group later became the prime suspects in the murders.

Dessie Hilton is a relative of Boogie Hilton and his brother Trevor and has been connected to the extended Laurie family throughout his life. When Detective Senior Sergeant Kerry Johnson interviewed him in 2008, Dessie claimed that Ungie Laurie, Shortie Laurie, Jimmy O'Neill and Larry Charles arrived at a house in Toowoomba where he was staying and bragged about giving two women a good hiding down the bottom of the range.

Dessie said that he was aware that the gang was in the habit of taking young women out, giving them 'a hiding', raping them and then just leaving them where they had assaulted them. These types of events took place every weekend for a number of years. He thought that what happened to the two murder victims was no different.

In a statement he made to police in 1989, Dessie Hilton said that in 1974 he was staying with Donnie Laurie in the flat next door to Boogie Hilton.

Ten years later, in 1999, Dessie told a detective that Ungie Laurie, Shortie Laurie, Jimmy O'Neill and Larry Charles were responsible for the murders of the two nurses, and that Donnie Laurie and Boogie Hilton went to Murphy's Creek to confirm that the victims were dead. Dessie claimed that the morning after the murders Ungie, Shortie, Jimmy and Larry arrived in a green-and-white EH Holden belonging to a member of the Laurie family. Dessie said that the men were in a hurry to clean up the vehicle and he had helped them. While the vehicle was being cleaned, Donnie Laurie and Boogie Hilton returned to Murphy's Creek. Dessie said that when they came back, Donnie had blood on him and went and cleaned himself up.

During an interview with the police in 2008, Dessie gave a further statement confirming the information he had given in 1989 and adding the following:

- He was well aware that the men were known to take women, give them a 'hiding', rape them and then, once they had got what they wanted from them, discard the victims — leave them where they had been assaulted. The morning after the murders, when the four men talked about having given the two women a 'good hiding', Dessie thought this meant that the gang had done what they had done every weekend for years to other victims.

- Donnie Laurie later told Dessie that at the crime scene he had taken a ring from one of the victims and subsequently sold it for beer at the Fiveways pub.
- Shortie Laurie was seen demonstrating to Donnie Laurie how he had assaulted the victims by kicking and stomping on the floor.

While giving evidence at the inquest, Dessie Hilton tried to retract many of these statements. However, he did confirm that Shortie Laurie was known for violence and described two incidents when he assaulted his own mother.

At the inquest Dessie was informed that he was still considered a suspect and could still be charged as an accessory after the fact, because he had admitted that he had cleaned up the blood in the Holden.

Daryl Sutton lived in Toowoomba in the 1970s. He was familiar with the Laurie and Hilton families and socialised with Boogie Hilton and Shortie Laurie. Daryl Sutton claimed to have witnessed Boogie act violently and attack both males and females on multiple occasions, including hitting young women on the face and body. He said Boogie was well known for being a 'girl basher' and that he hid a tyre lever under the driver's seat of the car. He also said that Boogie had a tattoo of a snake on his left forearm; however, on the police profile, there is only a note of a tattoo on Boogie's right bicep (of a heart with his wife's name, Roylene).

Trevor Hilton was both an uncle and cousin of Boogie Hilton. Trevor gave evidence that on multiple occasions, he witnessed Shortie and Ungie Laurie and Boogie Hilton bashing women and forcing them into cars. If they couldn't get them inside the vehicle, they would throw them into the boot. He also confirmed that the three men were known to carry tyre levers, wheel spanners and baseball bats in their vehicles to use as weapons against their unsuspecting victims, and that the men bragged about assaulting and raping women.

Kenneth Insley lived in Toowoomba periodically. He was 13 years old when the nurses were murdered and first met Donnie Laurie around the time that their remains were discovered. Despite the difference in their ages — Donnie Laurie was in his late 20s at the time — they would drink and go to parties together. He also began to associate with Trevor Hilton. Insley told the inquest that on one occasion Donnie Laurie and Trevor Hilton took him to the site where the two nurses' bodies were found. He said that the two men were laughing and boasting about the murders, and that he got frightened and asked them to get him out of there. As they drove back to Toowoomba, the men continued to talk about the two murdered nurses and Insley said he feared for his safety. He said Donnie Laurie said to him, 'You'll be more than frightened.'

He also testified that on one occasion, when Donnie Laurie and Trevor Hilton had been drinking to the point of intoxication, they began to argue. When Trevor said that he and Donnie were responsible for the murders of the nurses — 'We screwed them and killed them' — Donnie began shouting, 'Shut up'.

Insley said he asked where the incident took place and claimed Trevor told him it was on the dirt road to the right going down to Murphy's Creek Road. When Trevor began to go into detail, Insley tried to stop him, saying he didn't want to hear what took place. He said that Donnie became very upset and began to cry as a result of what Trevor was saying.

Insley said that Donnie Laurie later threatened him and his ex-wife with violence, saying, 'If you say anything about the murders at Murphy's Creek, I'll kill you too, and Betty.'

In October 1988, when Insley was an inmate at Long Bay Prison in Malabar, New South Wales, he gave a statement to a detective alleging that in 1984, while he was in Palen Creek Prison in Queensland, Trevor Hilton had told him that he and Donnie Laurie had killed two people.

Peter Tralka made a statement to the police in 1989 describing events that occurred when he and two mates were driving their car along the down-hill section of the Toowoomba Range Road one afternoon. Just before dark, he said, they witnessed two vehicles parked off on the left-hand side of the road. He identified the vehicles as a green EK Holden which Boogie Hilton owned and a grey EJ Holden which he recognised as belonging to associates of Hilton. As they drove past the two parked vehicles, Tralka said that he saw a person he believed to be Boogie Hilton on the ground struggling with another person, who was resisting. (He admitted to only seeing the aggressor from behind but believed that it was Boogie Hilton because of the vehicle and the dark wavy hair.) Tralka also said that another male was struggling with someone else closer to the green EK Holden. His friend Donald Collins, who also witnessed the incident, told Tralka that he thought the second aggressor was Shortie Laurie. Tralka could not confirm whether the people being restrained were male or female, but he felt that they were female.

He thought that he also saw a woman sitting in the EK sedan at the time of the incident.

Tralka and his friends saw the two vehicles driving down to the bottom of the range. They followed at a safe distance to see what was happening and saw the two cars go a short distance and then turn left into a paddock that was once used as a swimming area. At this point Tralka and his friends turned around and drove back to Toowoomba. Questioned by the coroner why they did not try to help the victims, Tralka said that they were too concerned about their own personal safety. He said, 'There were two car loads of them and only three of us.'

The coroner described Tralka's evidence as unreliable.

Neil Shum was a manager at a sawmill in Highfields in Toowoomba where Boogie Hilton had been employed on and off between the mid 1970s and early 1980s.

In 1989, three years after Boogie's death, Shum gave police a statement about the murder of the two nurses. He claimed that on numerous occasions Boogie had admitted that he was one of the people who had killed the two nurses who were found at Murphy's Creek. According to the statement, Boogie told Shum that he and his brother — Shum assumed he was talking about Trevor Hilton — picked up two nurses and 'had a bit of trouble with them and ended up murdering them'.

According to Shum, on one occasion, Boogie said, 'Did you see the picture of the cars in the paper? ... Owing to them cars ... they're onto us. ... You would have heard of the nurses being murdered a bit over the range?' Shum said that at the time of the murders Boogie Hilton drove a green EJ Holden with a white top and an EH Holden the same colour.

Walter Laurie is the younger brother of Shortie Laurie, the cousin of Boogie Hilton and the step-nephew of Ungie Laurie. At the time of the murders he was ten years old. In 2000 Walter gave the police a statement claiming that he witnessed the two nurses being assaulted by a group of his relatives and their friends.

On the night of the murder Shortie, Ungie, Boogie, Larry Charles, Donnie Laurie, Jimmy O'Neill and a man he referred to as 'Kingsley' Hunt came to Walter's family home in Toowoomba for a party with two women they had picked up in Goondiwindi. At around sunset the men drove down to Murphy's Creek with the nurses. Walter said that, with his mother Joyce and uncle Billy, he was in the car driven by his father Cecil. They drove down a bush track and stopped the car. His mother waited in the vehicle while his father and uncle Billy climbed through a barbed wire fence and walked through the bush into a clearing where there was a bonfire. They met up with Ungie, Shortie, Boogie, Donnie, Jimmy, Larry, Kingsley Hunt and William Baker. Another car drove up with some other men. Walter said that he saw his brother

Shortie's blue EH Holden and Ungie's green HR Holden at the scene.

According to his statement, he witnessed men, including Shortie, raping the two nurses. Walter said that he sat on a log watching what was going on for a while when Shortie came over and sat beside him. He said the taller woman yelled out 'That's enough', and saw the other woman 'knocked and pushed' to the ground by Ungie when she tried to get up. Walter heard the women begging for the men to stop.

This action triggered their father getting into a fight with Shortie. They left when his mother came into the clearing.

In 2000, after his statement was taken by police and 26 years after the murders, Walter returned to the murder site with police. He led them to the spot where he said he had witnessed the rapes. This was only the second time he had visited Murphy's Creek.

At the inquest, Walter was asked why he hadn't come forward with information earlier. He said that he had been concerned for his own safety. The reason he was telling police now, he said, was because he did not want to see the murdering bastards get away with the murders.

Albert Galvin was a friend of Donnie Laurie and also knew other members of the Laurie and Hilton families. He was interviewed by police in 1995 and claimed that, on his deathbed in Toowoomba Hospital, Donnie made a confession about the murders of the two nurses. Galvin claimed Donnie told him that the car involved in the murders was a green-and-white 1963 Ford Falcon, with blinds on the back windscreen, and that a tomahawk was used in the murders. He said there were three or four carloads of people involved and once again the names Ungie Laurie, Shortie Laurie and Boogie Hilton were mentioned.

Galvin confirmed the deathbed confession in a statement he made to police in 1996.

Desmond Edmondstone came forward as a witness because of media reports about the second inquest in 2013. Edmondstone, who was born in Texas, Queensland, is related to the Laurie family. Shortie Laurie is his first cousin and is ten years older. Edmondstone said he did not have a lot to do with Shortie when he was growing up, although he was mates with Shortie's younger brother, who went by the nickname of 'Strawberry' Laurie. In 1975, when he was about 16 years old, Edmondstone lived with the Laurie family in Toowoomba for about four months. He left shortly after, he said, because Shortie assaulted him and threatened to kill him in an unprovoked attack when he was sick in bed with the flu — he was bashed so severely that his cheekbones were broken.

Edmondstone reported that in 1978, he travelled north with Larry Charles and two friends to look for work. Along the way they decided to stay in Rockhampton at the caravan park and work at the local meat works before moving on. According to Edmondstone, while there Larry Charles said that it was two years to the day since 'those Murphy's Creek women' were killed and 'he was there'. Larry said they had picked up the two nurses while they were hitch-hiking in Toowoomba and that they had taken a 'big heap of grog to have a party' at Murphy's Creek. They were having a good time drinking and laughing.

Larry claimed, Edmondstone said, that the women consented to have sex with Shortie Laurie and Boogie Hilton. Jimmy O'Neill became angry when both the nurses said no to having sex with the other men. Boogie walked up to one of the women and hit her, then said, 'There you go, Jimmy, you can have your turn.' When one of the women ran off into the bush screaming, Boogie and Shortie chased after her while the other men grabbed the other woman. According to Larry, it took some time before they caught the woman who had escaped the men. When they got her back to the car, Boogie gave her a hiding.

A short time later Ungie Laurie and Dessie Hilton arrived with a number of other men. Larry said the men took turns raping and bashing the two nurses for hours on end — instead of drinking beer that night, he drank rum to make himself pass out because he couldn't stand to see what was going on. He said that the men partied all night and that it was the longest night of his life.

Larry told Edmondstone that after the murders, Donnie Laurie made the men make a blood-brothers pact that if anyone divulged what took place, the others had the right to kill them.

Edmondstone claimed that Larry had rung him one night out of the blue and said he had spoken to a priest about what happened and that the priest had told him to confess the crime to the police. He asked Edmondstone what he thought he should do. Edmondstone said that he told Larry that the only way he would ever be clear was when he was dead. The following day Larry Charles shot himself.

Kim Sandercock made a statement to police in 1989 about an incident she said occurred at the Crown Hotel, Toowoomba in 1984. One afternoon when she was sitting at a table by herself, an intoxicated woman who she did not know sat down and told her a story about a man Kim presumed the woman was living with.

The woman said her name was 'Ellen' but would not give her surname. She said she was tired of covering up something that she was not involved in. Then she talked about the Murphy's Creek murders. Ellen, who the police have not been able to identify, said she was present when the two nurses were murdered but did not take an active part. According to Sandercock, the woman said that two men were involved in killing the nurses — one was Allan Laurie (Ungie) and the other was one of the Hilton boys.

Ellen said that the two men had picked up the women and thought that they were 'prick teasers' because they did not want to have sex with them. The men intended to rape the nurses, not to murder them. One of the nurses sat in the front of the vehicle and the other was sitting in the back between Ellen and the other man.

According to Sandercock, Ellen said that when the woman in the front seat tried to escape from the car, the man sitting in the back hit her with a bar on the back of the head. The blow caused her to fall forward and her head began to bleed profusely. Ellen said that she thought that the woman was dead. The woman in the back began to scream so they put a gag in her mouth. They then dumped the dead body of the nurse in the bush. The second nurse tried to escape and the men ran after her. When they caught her, they pulled out some of her hair. Ellen said the men were more vicious with her because she was causing them trouble. She was hit with something and her head was bashed in. After she was dead, the men dragged her body back to near where the first victim's body lay.

Kim Sandercock said that she was shaken and quite shocked by what Ellen told her. When she stood up to leave the table, Ellen grabbed hold of her and said that if she ever told anybody about the story, she would end up the same way as the murdered nurses.

Arriving at the inquest in a wheelchair hooked up to a morphine drip, Kim Sandercock insisted that the use of painkillers had damaged her memory of the conversation with Ellen. The coroner was frustrated, accusing her of concocting a mystery female witness and of lying about her poor memory due to her fears. He felt it was more likely that she was either present during the murder or that someone she knew had described the events to her. The information that she gave about the injuries to the women's bodies was not published at the time she made her first statement.

◎   ◎   ◎

On 28 June 2013, the Queensland state coroner, Michael Barnes, found that Wendy Joy Evans and Lorraine Ruth Wilson 'died on 6 or 7 October 1974 ... at or near Murphy's Creek via Helidon in Queensland.' They 'both died as a result of head wounds intentionally inflicted by or in the presence of Wayne Robert Hilton and one or more persons who cannot be sufficiently identified.'

The second inquest did uncover new evidence, but unfortunately nobody has been charged with the murders. I am sure the family members of Wendy Joy Evans and Lorraine Ruth Wilson have mixed feelings about the outcome. I certainly do. It is so disgusting that a group of cowardly men banded together, inflicting such a reign of terror during the 1970s, and were able to get away with their crimes. At least now the true story of what happened to the two nurses on that terrible night at Murphy's Creek has been revealed. It is such a shame that the many witnesses who saw what happened to the women didn't come forward sooner.

Some of the men named as suspects are dead and will never be brought to justice. One positive outcome from the inquest was that one of the perpetrators, Wayne Boogie Hilton was named, even if posthumously.

Journalist Michael Usher tried to interview two of the suspects on a *60 Minutes* television program. The story, called 'Murder at Murphy's Creek' which aired on 2 March 2014, was interesting to watch because the hunters now felt that they were being hunted. I hope that the perpetrators will one day be brave enough to give themselves up to police and be charged for their crimes.

◎   ◎   ◎

I have spoken to Eric Wilson, Lorraine's brother, about the murders. I can't even begin to imagine the torment that he and his family have been through. It was a major task for Eric and his mother to have a public coronial inquest into Lorraine and Wendy's death.

Due to the inquest, at least one protagonist was named, suspects were revealed and families were shamed.

Before the second inquest took place, Betty Wilson had written to Michael Barnes, the state coroner, asking to have the case reopened. Only three days later she died in a tragic farming accident, so did not learn that her request for an inquest was granted.

RETURN TO MURPHY'S CREEK, 2015

In November 2015, I was contacted by CP International, a Japanese television production company, and asked if I was interested in discussing my psychic detective work for their series called *Goosebumps*. We agreed that the case I would focus on was the Murphy's Creek murders. I felt that this would give the case more exposure and give the victims a voice on an international level.

Most importantly, I needed to ask Eric Wilson, Lorraine's brother, for his permission to work on the case with the television production crew. Eric declined to be involved because he didn't want to revisit the trauma of what had happened to his baby sister Lorraine and her best friend Wendy. Eric gave me his blessing to work on the case. He knew how much it had haunted me and said he hoped that I would find my own inner peace and find closure as he had at the end of the second inquest into the murders.

I hoped too that by travelling to Toowoomba and Murphy's Creek with the film crew, I would be able to fill in more of the missing pieces about what happened to the nurses on that day in 1974, as well as finally be able to put this case to bed.

Goosebumps features three psychic detectives from around the world — one from Russia, one from the USA and me from Australia.

Day 1 of filming. The Japanese film crew were lovely, even though we had to overcome a few language barriers. We met at my office in Sutherland where I did an interview introducing the case. The crew decided that they should film at my home, so that I could be interviewed about the case and tune in to the victims. I used a photograph to make contact and it didn't take long for the nurses to make their presence known. Again, Lorraine was the most vocal of the two and communicated with me the strongest.

After we recorded the interviews, we arranged to meet at Sydney Airport early the following morning to go to Toowoomba and revisit the crime scene.

I found it very hard to sleep that night. The energy of the two women was overwhelming. Lorraine kept me awake, telling me how excited she was about me going back to Toowoomba with her. She was pleased that she and Wendy would have more exposure about their plight and she hoped that somewhere, somehow, someone would find new information that may help to solve the case. I was up very early, feeling very wound up about the day ahead. I joked with the crew that I hoped that it wasn't going to be too hot because the crime scene was quite bushy and I hoped we wouldn't be meeting any snakes there.

Once in Toowoomba, we had some lunch and discussed the next two days of filming. While we were eating, lots of beautiful butterflies kept flying around our table. I suddenly heard Lorraine telling me that the butterflies were a sign from her and Wendy. She said that I needed to pay attention to butterflies during our stay in Toowoomba — they would be important.

Ken, the producer, said that he had been in town just the week before. Apparently, the motel we were staying in was built on the grounds of the town's old gaol and the café where we were having lunch was the site of the hospital at the women's gaol. This was going to make for an interesting evening when we returned from the murder site.

It was about 20 minutes' drive to Murphy's Creek. I felt excitement and foreboding. I could feel the presence of Lorraine and Wendy sitting in the car we were travelling in. I was pleased that both of them had found me — the journey we were embarking on was an extremely important moment for us all. This trip was so different from the first time I had been to Murphy's Creek. I knew more of the pieces of the puzzle than last time. However, that knowledge was more horrific than I had imagined the first time I'd been here.

As we drove along, I felt as if I had become Lorraine. I could feel my heart racing. I could feel the despair the women felt about how they couldn't get out of the situation they were in. I could see how Lorraine was thinking and planning ways for her and Wendy to escape. Lorraine wondered if there was anything she could say to the perpetrators to convince them to stop and let them go.

We turned onto Murphy's Creek Road. I could feel tears welling up in my eyes. I felt so upset about the women's fate that I found it hard to control my emotions.

Murphy's Creek Road is still quite rural. There are farmhouses along the side of the road, thinning out the further you drive. One section of the road runs alongside the railway line. I had a distinct memory of passing a train station at Murphy's Creek when I was filming the *Sensing Murder* episode.

Driving past the station and signal box, the emotions were quite overwhelming. I knew that we were getting close. Suddenly, I was taken back in time and I could see and hear Wendy and Lorraine pleading with the perpetrators to let them out at the station so that they could catch the train home. I could hear laughter as the men told them that there was no way they were going to let them go. They were going to a party and the nurses were the entertainment whether they liked it or not. I could feel the anguish and desperation that was building within the women. I could see Lorraine working out ways for them to escape. I could see where the car had pulled over and I was amazed to see how other vehicles would have been able to see the car and how they witnessed the nurses yelling and pleading for someone to stop and help them. A number of cars drove past them but nobody came to their assistance.

I felt as if I was in a nightmare, only the nightmare wasn't happening to me. I was a psychic witness watching helplessly and I was not able to save the people in this terrible dream. I knew that part of working on this case meant being part of the story — seeing this horrific tragedy unfold before my eyes so that I could help to fill in the missing pieces. Seeing and hearing what the nurses went through was such an emotional drain on my own body. However, I knew that it was necessary to tell their story.

We drove a little farther down the road and then turned onto Stevens Road where the murders had taken place. It had been 11 years since I had been at the site and many things were different. At the turn-off there was a house that I didn't remember seeing before.

Something didn't look right. However, it certainly felt right. We stopped the car and I went for a walk into the bush. It was about 2.30 pm and the sun was beaming down. There was a 'For Sale' sign hanging crookedly off a timber stake. I saw barbed wire fencing and began to walk through the bush into a clearing. The burned logs and discarded beer cans were no longer there, but there were charred reminders of bushfires that had gone through the area some time ago. I walked a little farther into the bush but felt frustrated that I might not be in the exact spot. I stood there for a few minutes and then asked the crew if we could drive up the road a bit more, just in case I wasn't far enough up the road. We got back into the car. Stevens Road is partly tarred gravel, then turns into a dirt road.

I was looking for a long dirt track marked by a big gum tree on the right-hand side of Stevens Road, a scene featured on the cover of Eric Wilson's book *The Echo of Silent Screams: The Gold Coast Hitchhike Murders.*

A view of the dirt track at Murphy's Creek. Source: Queensland Police Service

As we drove up the road, I could see that there is now a property very close to the place I was looking for. There were discarded vehicles, machinery and car parts, as well as rubbish strewn along the roadside. The feeling was not very welcoming.

Just to be sure we were in the right location, we drove along to the beginning of the dirt road, although I felt that we had travelled too far. During the drive up the road I noticed that there were two more properties that had not been built at the time of the murders. The landscape became quite steep and at the top of the range I got out of the car to get my bearings. I felt that the first place we'd been was the right location. We went back to the 'For Sale' sign and I walked into the site, tuning in to Lorraine and Wendy via a photograph of them.

I stopped and closed my eyes, tuning in to the nurses' energy. The temperature was about 26 degrees Celsius. Initially, it was very still and the only sounds were of birds singing in the distance. Suddenly the energy shifted and I could feel that we were not alone anymore.

A breeze began to swirl around us and the temperature dropped a few degrees. As I opened my eyes, the two women stood before me. I could see them both very clearly.

I understood how hard it must have been for these beautiful women to return to the site of their murders. I couldn't even begin to understand how much pain and anguish they had suffered when they were here. What did surprise me though was the presence of Lorraine's mother Betty Wilson, standing by her daughter's side.

I have worked on a lot of murder cases and this is the first time I have seen a victim and a deceased parent together in this way. I took this as a very precious sign that Lorraine and Betty gave me their approval for what I was trying to do. I was overwhelmed by happiness that mother and daughter had finally reunited and that, despite the suffering they had both experienced during their lives, they were together again.

Lorraine and Wendy began to tell me what happened to them at the murder scene. They showed me where they were tied up and talked about who the perpetrators were. Lorraine asked me to follow her from the clearing and walk farther into the bush with her. She said she was taking me to a creek that was very close to where the murders had taken place. I found the creek, which was dried up — she said that she had tried to escape by running down to the creek bed, but one of the men caught her and dragged her back by the hair, while she was kicking and screaming.

Once Lorraine was taken back to the site, she said that the men hog-tied her and Wendy to stop any more escape attempts. I was explaining to the film crew what I was seeing and feeling when another presence appeared before me. I was in complete shock. I recognised this man to be Hilton, the man named in the second inquest as involved in the murder of the nurses.

Standing there with his head down, I saw that he was telling me that he was remorseful for what he did and said he had been haunted by what happened until his death. He kept repeating that he didn't want to kill the women, he said that he and the other men just wanted to have some fun. The situation got out of hand when more men joined the group, he said. Boogie wanted to have fun with the women and he didn't want to share them with the others.

He said that he got so drunk that he couldn't even remember how bad things became. It wasn't until the following day when he returned to the murder scene with one of the other men, he said, that he realised what they had done. I could hear him sobbing and I could see that he was feeling extremely sorry for himself.

All I could feel was total disgust for this man. I hoped that he felt remorseful, I hoped that he was upset at what he had done. I hoped that he felt raw guilt and that made it possible for him to understand what he had inflicted on these two innocent young women. Just as we were about to leave the site another man appeared. I recognised that he was the man named Larry Charles.

Larry Charles didn't say anything to me at first. He also stood in front of me, with his head in his hands, and he was also crying. He told me that he didn't hurt the women, he just wanted to have some fun with them. When things got out of hand, he wanted to help them, but was too frightened of what would happen to him. He said that he was weak — he was more worried about himself and his own safety. If he attempted to assist the girls, he said, he feared that he would also be bashed and possibly murdered like the nurses. He said that he hated himself for not doing anything to assist them. He said that his guilt overcame him so he ended his own life because he felt that he was a disgrace to himself and to the women.

In my vision the other man in the car on that fateful day was Allan Shortie Laurie. I was shown images of him and Boogie Hilton picking up the hitch-hikers and driving them up to the range on the day of the murders.

After filming all we needed for the episode, we stood at the murder site for a few minutes in silence. The five members of the film crew also felt something at the location. What is interesting is that all of the crew were Japanese and not all of them spoke English fluently — nevertheless, at that point we all connected on a spiritual level and all felt the deep sadness of what had taken place there.

Ken, the producer, said that the others could all feel the emotions of the women and that they felt touched by their presence. I felt that this was a way of Lorraine and Wendy thanking us for making the long trip to Murphy's Creek to tell their story and to ensure that they wouldn't be forgotten.

We drove back to our motel in silence and contemplated what we had just witnessed, as well as thinking about what the poor victims had gone through in the lonely bush clearing where they had been murdered. I did an interview about what I had just experienced at the murder scene. Lorraine and Wendy's presence was very strong in the room we were filming in. It was very reassuring to have them with us.

At the end of the interview I showed the crew how to film 'orbs' in the room. Orbs — balls of light that look like a full moon — are spirit energy of deceased people that show up on film and in photographs. They can vary in shape, size and colour, depending upon the energy of the person in spirit. They tend to reflect off the light of the camera flash or, if there is a constant light on the video camera or phone, they will show up on the recording. In this instance, I asked the nurses to show themselves on camera and they were both happy to oblige. First I tried with my iPhone, then the crew asked me if I would try to film them with their video camera.

We captured some very strong images of orbs on my iPhone and this made the crew very excited. The director, Yo Yo, asked if he could try to film the orbs on my phone himself as he wanted to see if they were more drawn to me than the phone.

Yo Yo then asked if I could leave the room so he could see if the orbs were as strong as when I was in the room. Interestingly, once I left the room the orb energy was not as strong and the orbs did not appear as frequently on the iPhone. When I came back into the room the orbs reappeared.

* * *

After we finished filming, we decided to go into town for dinner. It was a very interesting evening in downtown Toowoomba. Toowoomba is a large country town with a very Aussie vibe. When five Japanese men and one Australian woman walked into the restaurant, it was quite obvious that we didn't belong. Everyone seemed to be staring at us, especially at the camera crew who were speaking to each other in Japanese. I was having a wonderful time speaking with Show, the owner of the production team from Japan.

The crew asked me how I tune in and about the type of readings I do. I told them that I was a psychic medium and that I also did numerology. They asked if I could do their numerology — which was very interesting because most of the crew had very psychic and spiritual numbers. I asked them if they could see things. Yo Yo didn't speak English very well. However, through Ken interpreting we could have a conversation. Yo Yo had very psychic numbers and he said that he could see and feel spirits. At the murder site that day, he said, he could strongly feel that the nurses were there with us. He said that he could feel their sadness. Josh and Bob, the cameraman and soundman respectively, also had very psychic numbers and both of them said they could feel something at the murder site.

While sitting at dinner, for some unknown reason I was drawn to look at the watch Bob was wearing. It was black with a large digital face. I didn't know why I was so drawn to it, but I was told that it would make sense to me later. After dinner we headed back to the motel. I went to my room to get my camera so I could take some photographs of the old gaol next door. As I returned, I could see Josh standing outside his room looking very uncomfortable. Then Bob drove up and parked the van. Bob said that he had gone back to the restaurant because he had lost his watch and thought it may be there. I couldn't help smiling to myself — now I understood why I was drawn to look at his watch.

I suddenly saw an image of Bob putting his hand into his sound recording bag and the watch falling off into the bag. I told him that I was told to look at his watch at the restaurant and I knew that he hadn't lost it there. Bob went into his room and when he put his hand into the bag he found his watch inside. He came back with a big smile on his face and asked me how did I know that it was there. I just laughed and said, 'because they told me so, because I am psychic'.

Poor Josh was still standing uncomfortably outside his door. I asked him what was the matter and he said he saw a shadow walk past him in his room. I told him that I would go inside and check the room out and if necessary would clear it for him. As soon as I entered the room I could feel an unpleasant male spirit energy. I knew that the energy wasn't the nurses because their energy was soft and gentle. I walked into each of the rooms and cleared the spirit out. I took Josh outside and cleared his aura and taught him how to white light himself so that he would be able to sleep during the night.

Then I went to bed. Even though I had cleared my room and white lighted myself, the fact that we were sleeping on the grounds of an old gaol did make it a pretty interesting night. It seemed as if I was the lighthouse that all the lost souls were drawn to, so there wasn't much chance of getting a good night's sleep.

In the morning I asked everyone how their night was. Josh said he was fine, Bob was fine, Show slept like a log, Ken felt that there was a presence, but poor Yo Yo said his front door kept opening during the night. He would get up and close it and then it would open again. He said that he saw dark shadows walking around in the room and they kept him awake all night. I told him it was a shame that he didn't tell me sooner as I would have cleared the room for him.

The crew had an early start and left to film some scenes around the town of Toowoomba. Show and I had breakfast together and talked about what we had experienced over the last few days.

When the crew returned, they were very excited. Ken showed me a picture of the exact type of car that was used to pick up the nurses at the time of the murder. They had filmed a green EH Holden with a white roof and venetians in the back driving around in town. This is a vintage car that you don't normally see driving down the street. I took it as a sign from the young women that they were happy with what we were doing.

It was time for me to do another interview about what I had experienced during our two days in Toowoomba. While I was being interviewed in a park, a huge butterfly flew up to me, landed on my head, then flew off into the distance. I stopped speaking mid-sentence because I was shocked when I saw the flash of colour coming at my face. When I realised what had happened, you couldn't wipe the smile off my face. The whole crew began to smile and said that I had told them to keep an eye out for butterflies. Once again I felt that this was another sign that the nurses were happy with all that we had been doing and what we were trying to do on their behalf.

We returned to the motel for one last interview. I was asked to look at images of the suspects and to relay to the crew what I thought about each man. When I tuned in to the image I spoke about my feelings about each individual and whether or not he was at the crime scene and what his involvement was with the case.

The first man I looked at was Boogie Hilton. The images from the previous day came flooding back into my mind. The disgust I felt for this man was overwhelming. I relayed how I had seen him at the murder site the previous day and the emotional state that he presented before me. The worst part of it all was that he was more sorry for himself than he was for what had happened to the women. Yes, he said he was sorry, but unfortunately the feeling I got was more of how the event had affected his life, not those of the victims and their families. To be honest, I could feel absolutely no pity for this man — all I could feel was total anger. Boogie Hilton seems to have got away with the murder of two innocent young women, and whether he was remorseful was of no interest to me. All I could think about was the two beautiful nurses whose lives he had cut short, not to mention the suffering that he inflicted on them both.

I continued watching each clip of the six suspected murderers and then gave my thoughts about whether they were involved and in what capacity.

While watching the clip of Allan Shortie Laurie, I was immediately taken back in time and could see him in the car with Boogie Hilton. This man had eyes that could turn cold as ice when he was on the attack. In my psychic visions, he was one of the main perpetrators and one of the original men who picked up the two nurses in the green-and-white EH Holden. He had a way of convincing the women that they were in safe hands and that the men would give them a good time.

While we were at the murder location the previous day, I saw visions of Shortie Laurie taking turns raping the women. He seemed to be really enjoying himself, sitting around the bonfire with the 'gang' drinking beer and then attacking the women. This man was one of the ring leaders.

Larry Charles seemed to be the only man I saw in my visions who was remorseful about what had happened to the women. I did see him at the murder scene; however, I don't feel that he was as bad as the other perpetrators. That being said, he was there and he could have done more to protect the nurses. He did tell me that he was frightened for his own safety. Being a coward is no excuse for allowing what happened to the women, of course. It is such a shame that he didn't have the guts to go to the police and tell the truth about what happened on that fateful night before he killed himself.

I could see that Donnie Laurie was at the murder site; however, I felt that he joined the group later in another vehicle. I could see him sitting around the bonfire drinking. I could see that he participated in the gang rape of the two young women. He was the oldest of the six suspects — you would have hoped that he wouldn't have encouraged the men's behaviour. However, I could see that he did encourage them. He found it entertaining to watch what the other men did to the nurses.

As we were travelling back to Brisbane to catch our flight to Sydney, we talked about what we had just experienced together. The entire crew were in shock as to why these murders hadn't been solved. They had gone through all the research and had interviewed other people to do with the murders — and they were at a loss to explain why there were men still living their lives freely when it was clear that they were part of the gang that murdered the two young nurses.

After returning to Toowoomba and revisiting the murder site, I felt exactly the same way. All I could honestly say is that I was disappointed that more wasn't done at the time of the murders and that, even though there have been two inquests, no-one has been arrested for the murders. The policing at the time of the murders certainly had some shortfalls.

I was pleased though that I had the opportunity to return to the site after all these years. It gave me a new perspective on things. I feel that I have achieved an inner peace by connecting with the two beautiful young women before going to Toowoomba and, most importantly, at the murder site. Seeing them appear before me and also seeing Lorraine's mother joining them there is something I will never forget. I felt blessed to have experienced the reunion, and despite what they had all gone through, it was wonderful to see that they were together again in spirit.

⊚　⊚　⊚

Nothing will ever change what happened to Lorraine Wilson and Wendy Evans, at least now Betty Wilson knows that her daughter will not be forgotten and they are reunited in spirit.

My greatest wish is for Eric Wilson to now be able to lay the torment of what happened to his sister and to Wendy to rest. The women cannot be brought back; however, through Eric and his mother's efforts, the young nurses did have a voice and finally somebody listened.

The final message from Lorraine to Eric is: 'Thank you, I love you, big brother. It is now your time to live for all of us. Don't hold back — when you have joy, we feel it too. Mum is safe and well and we are reunited with Wendy. When the wind-chimes chime it is a sign we are near. This is not goodbye — it is until we meet again. Your loving little sister, Lorraine.'

I also hope that the proposed memorial plaque for Lorraine and Wendy that was promised to the family by the Toowoomba Council will finally be erected in a city park. It seems that some members of the council still want to forget what happened that day. The memorial should be erected so that people remember what happened to two innocent young women and in the hope that no other person or family has to endure a similar experience in the future.

⊚　⊚　⊚

I wish to thank Eric Wilson for allowing me to tell his sister's story and for all of his assistance and support during my second visit to Toowoomba. Thank you for allowing me to share your beautiful sister's story. Eric, you are a truly brave and courageous man I am blessed to have met.

Eric Wilson is the author of two books detailing the Murphy's Creek murders: The Echo of Silent Screams: The Gold Coast Hitchhike Murders *and* The Ricochet of Echoes: The Lorraine Wilson and Wendy Evans Murders. *The books are available through Amazon.*

Chapter 3

What Happened to Bob Chappell?

NAME: Robert Adrian Chappell (known as Bob)

MISSING SINCE: 26 January 2009

LAST SEEN: Hobart,
   Tasmania

DATE OF BIRTH: 2
   February 1943

AGE AT DISAPPEARANCE:
   65

BUILD: Slim

HAIR: Grey, balding

EYES: Blue

COMPLEXION: Fair.

Bob Chappell. Source: Eve Ash

Robert Adrian (Bob) Chappell was last seen alive on Australia Day, 26 January 2009, by his partner Sue Neill-Fraser. Bob vanished while working on the couple's yacht *Four Winds* while it was moored in Sandy Bay, just off the Royal Yacht Club.

On 20 August 2009 Sue Neill-Fraser was charged with Bob's murder. She was found guilty and sentenced to 26 years' imprisonment, with no parole until she had served 18 years. (The sentence was later reduced to 23 years with a minimum of 13 years.) The most baffling thing about this is that Bob's body has never been found and the case was based on circumstantial evidence.

The Bob Chappell case is one of Australia's greatest mysteries. Sue Neill-Fraser's conviction, based entirely on circumstantial evidence, has been likened to the Lindy Chamberlain case.

◎　　◎　　◎

Bob Chappell was the chief radiation physicist at the Royal Hobart Hospital's Holman Clinic. Bob was born in England on 2 February 1943 and was 65 at the time of his disappearance. Sue Neill-Fraser, who was born in Scotland on 3 March 1954, was 55 when Bob went missing.

The couple lived together in Allison Street, West Hobart. Both had adult children from their first marriages: Bob had Timothy, Kate and Clare, and Sue was the mother of Emma and Sarah. Sue and Bob had been in a de-facto relationship for 18 years when he disappeared.

In September 2008 the couple purchased *Four Winds*, a 16-metre ketch, for $203,000 from a broker at the Scarborough Marina, Queensland. *Four Winds* required work on the engine before being sailed to Hobart. On 7 December, Bob and Sue began the journey to Hobart with two crew members, Peter Stevenson and David Casson. The trip was eventful. Early on, Bob suffered a nosebleed. Then, approaching Southport on the second day, the engine failed and the coastguard was called to tow the yacht into Southport.

In Southport, Bob's nosebleed persisted and he subsequently was admitted to hospital. The two crew members were concerned about Bob's health and so it was decided that he would fly to Hobart while Sue, Peter and David continued to sail the yacht on to Hobart. The *Four Winds* arrived in Hobart late on the evening of 23 December. During the sail to Hobart there had been a number of mechanical and equipment failures.

On 25 January 2009, Sue, Bob and his sister Caroline Ann Sanchez (the family called her Ann) spent the day cruising to Bruny Island and back. They did not attempt to sail, choosing to motor there and back. When they arrived at Bruny Island the anchor winch failed, so they were unable to lower the anchor. According to Ann, Bob and Sue wrestled with the winch and Bob was grumpy about its failure. He had said, 'Look, I'm beginning to wonder about this boat. What else is going to go wrong with it?'

On 26 January at around 8.30 to 9.30 am, Bob and Sue returned to the *Four Winds* on its mooring, using the dinghy to access the yacht. While on the yacht, Bob was constantly in and out of the engine room doing repairs and had an electrical switchboard open.

Bob stayed working on the yacht when Sue, who was planning to have lunch with Ann, used the dinghy to return to shore and tied it up to poles at the Marieville Esplanade. On shore Sue drove back to the Allison Street house so she could get changed, pick up Ann and take her to the Royal Yacht

Club for lunch. After lunch Sue returned to the house and changed again, leaving there at 1.30 pm. Ann went to Bruny Island that afternoon to spend two days there.

At approximately 1.30 to 2 pm at Short Beach, Christopher Liaubon helped Sue to free the dinghy's outboard motor — the tide was about three-quarters of the way out and it was stuck in the sand above the waterline. Once it was freed Sue motored out to the *Four Winds*.

A number of witnesses saw a grey dinghy tied to the *Four Winds* at about 3.55 pm and at 5.30 pm.

Sue spent a short time on the yacht with Bob while he worked in the engine room and on the anchor winch motor. He told Sue that he had isolated an engine oil leak and wanted to spend the night on board so he could keep working on it. He wanted to trace the wiring and have a look at things. Sue left her mobile phone with Bob and left the *Four Winds* in the dinghy. She said she had been on the yacht for about an hour at the most. Sue tied the dinghy to a ladder at the yacht club with three knots in her usual way. She believed that it was tied up adequately as it had never come undone before.

Sue went back to the house in Allison Street. At 9.17 pm she made a 14-minute phone call to her daughter Emma Mills on the landline. Then she rang her mother and talked for about five minutes. At 10.05 pm Sue received a phone call from a stranger called Richard King, which lasted approximately 29 minutes. King tells Sue that Bob's daughter Clare thinks that something bad will happen to Bob while he is on the yacht. The next time the Allison Street landline was used was at 3.08 am the following morning. It was a *10# call to retrieve the number of the last unanswered phone call to the house.

Sue Neill-Fraser and Bob
Chappell. Source: Eve Ash

John Hughes was parked at the end of the rowing shed at Marieville Esplanade, Sandy Bay, between 11.30 pm and midnight when he saw an inflatable dinghy coming from the direction of the yacht club. He said that the dinghy was heading in a northeasterly direction, towards the eastern shore of the Derwent River. He thought there was only one person on board the dinghy and he felt by the outline of the figure that it was female —he could not be definite about this though. He said that there were no other people in the area at the time. However, police interviewed a homeless man who was living there in his car at the time.

At about 5.40 am on 27 January the yacht's dinghy was found floating and nudging up against the rocks in a small cove several hundred metres away from where Sue had tied it up the previous day. The dinghy's painter — the line that anchors it to a dock or to a boat and is also used for towing or anchoring — was positioned inside the dinghy, which indicated that someone had untied the dinghy from where Sue had secured it. If the dinghy had come undone and simply drifted away, it is most unlikely that the painter would have been inside the dinghy — it was more likely to be trailing in the water.

At 7.04 am an unanswered phone call was made from the Allison Street landline to Sue's mobile phone, which she had left with Bob on the *Four Winds*. Seven minutes later, at 7.11 am, Sue was phoned by police and notified that the *Four Winds* was sinking. Bob Chappell was missing. He has never been seen again.

◉ ◉ ◉

THE TIMELINE

Australia Day, 26 January 2009

7 am: Caroline Ann Sanchez (known as Ann), Bob's sister, is staying with Bob and Sue at their home in Allison Street, West Hobart. This is the last time that Ann sees Bob alive.

8 am: Bob and Sue take the dinghy to the *Four Winds*, which is on its mooring in Sandy Bay.

9 am: Bob undertakes work on the yacht. There is a problem with the electrics and he is trying to trace the issue.

11 am: Sue uses the dinghy to get to shore for a lunch engagement with Bob's sister Ann at the Royal Yacht Club.

12 pm: Sue meets Ann.

1.04 pm: Sue makes an 11–second phone call to Bunnings.

1.10 pm: Sue takes Ann back to the Allison Street house. She then drives back to the foreshore and parks her vehicle.

1.30 pm: Christopher Liaubon helps Sue to free the dinghy's outboard motor at Sandy Bay.

2.00 pm: Sue returns to the *Four Winds* in the dinghy. She is at the yacht for approximately an hour and Bob stays alone on board. Sue leaves her mobile phone with Bob because he has decided to stay overnight to continue tracing the electrical issue on the yacht.

3.55 pm: According to a witness, Paul Conde, a 'large grey dinghy' is tied up to the *Four Winds*. It is a dark grey/charcoal colour and has a grey lee cloth over its bow. (The sighting of the grey dinghy was also confirmed by another witness on a yacht.)

5.00 pm: A witness, referred to as 'P36' at Sue's trial, sees a 'large mid grey' inflatable dinghy tied up to the *Four Winds*. The witness's companion notes that the yacht is 'sitting low in the water'.

7.45-8.30 pm: A local resident witnesses a 'weather-beaten' man in a dinghy with an outboard in the vicinity of the *Four Winds*.

9.17 pm: Sue makes a phone call to her daughter Emma and then calls her mother from her home.

10.05-10.34 pm: Sue receives a phone call from a stranger by the name of Richard King which lasts for approximately 29 minutes. King tells Sue that Bob's daughter Clare thinks that something bad will happen to Bob while he is on the yacht and that it will sink.

10.35-11.40 pm: Richard King contacts Timothy Chappell and gives him the same message.

11 pm-1.30 am: A local woman hears a 'distressed mature male voice'.

11.30 pm-12.00 am: A witness, named John Hughes, sees a dinghy travelling approximately 50 metres off the point near the rowing shed carpark. Hughes thought he saw the 'outline of a woman' in the dinghy.

27 January 2009

12.25 am: Footage from an ATM shows a blurred image of a car, which police suggest is Sue's, travelling north along Sandy Bay Road. The image is blurred and it is impossible to see the vehicle's make, model and number plate.

Early hours: Sue is worried after King's call and walks down to the foreshore at Marieville Esplanade, Sandy Bay, where she left her car, so she can take it home to West Hobart. While near the rowing sheds, Sue said she noticed several homeless people around a fire.

3.08 am: Sue arrives home. She dials *10# to access any missed calls.

5.40 am: The dinghy from the *Four Winds* is found untethered against rocks off the rowing shed carpark.

7 am: Port Control Marine contact local police about a yacht sinking off Sandy Bay. Police arrive with a local salvage company to try and re-float the yacht.

7.11 am: Sue receives a phone call from police telling her that the *Four Winds* is sinking. She heads to the yacht club in her car.

7.30 am: Sue arrives at the Royal Yacht Club where police and media are gathering.

8.45 am: The yacht is pumped out and stabilised and later towed to Constitution Dock.

8.53 am: A forensics team is requested to attend the yacht to take samples on board the yacht.

10.10 am: A red waterproof jacket similar to those used by yachtsmen is located on a fence at 2 Margaret Street, Sandy Bay, by the occupant of the house.

4.30 pm: Sue and family members board the yacht at Constitution Dock. Sue notices that a number of things are out of place or missing, including the EPIRB (emergency position indicating radio beacon) and fire extinguisher, and that there is a torch, juice bottle and other drink containers that she does not recognise. She notes that ropes had been cut and that the winch handle was in the wrong location.

5 pm: Police attempt to hand the *Four Winds* back to Sue. Sue declines and insists that police undertake further forensic examination.

5.30 pm: Police Forensic Services are requested to attend the *Four Winds* for further examination.

6.15 pm: Further checks are made by police in regard to any activation of any EPIRB because the *Four Winds'* EPIRB is missing.

WHAT I SAW PSYCHICALLY

In April 2011, I received a phone call from Eve Ash. Eve is a psychologist, author and filmmaker who runs her own production company called Seven Dimensions. She asked if I would be interested in assisting her with a missing person's case. I agreed, so we decided to meet up at my office in Sutherland on Monday, 2 May. I told Eve that I didn't want to know anything about the case before our meeting.

I had asked Eve to bring some photographs and personal items of the missing person for me to tune in to during our reading. When she arrived with her film crew, I was introduced to a young woman by the name of Sarah. Sarah was related to the missing person and it was through her and the items that I attempted to make contact.

After the crew were set up, I began the reading by tuning in to a pipe and a photograph of an older man, who I was told was named Robert Chappell. From the moment I began to tune in, I could hear and see Bob, which indicated to me that he was no longer alive. In the picture, Bob was standing at the helm of his yacht with his beloved pipe in his shirt pocket. When I saw this image I was given the impression that he absolutely loved this boat — it seemed to be something of an achievement for him to own it.

By holding the items, I was given psychic impressions of what had happened to Bob. I received a sharp stabbing pain to my right side and right shoulder. The pain felt as if I had been stabbed by a knife. I also felt a very hard thump to the rear of my head on the right side. The pain was very intense, causing me to immediately have a headache. While tuning in to cases, I find that the pain and suffering the victim underwent during death can be quite a drain on my own body physically as I experience the pain. During this stage of making contact with the victim, I have to really focus because the pain can be so overwhelming that I lose focus on the information I am being shown.

Bob had very interesting energy. He came across as a very impatient man who could be described as rather grumpy. He told me that he had a lot of frustration about what happened to him and I could feel his anger boiling up within me. All he wanted was for the truth to be known.

I got the impression that Bob was a man who was used to being listened to — he had a certain authority about him. He didn't suffer fools gladly and he could rub people up the wrong way. Bob was a very intelligent man, who found it difficult to relate to people who didn't understand his way of thinking. He was a perfectionist who found it hard to trust others to do a job as well as he thought he could. Bob had a problem with speaking first and not necessarily thinking later about what he had said, which alienated him from some people.

As I tuned in further to Bob, he began to tell me how worried he was about his partner. During the reading, I came to understand that his partner Sue had been gaoled for 26 years for Bob's murder. What was very unusual about this case was that Bob's body has never been found. Sarah, the young woman I was doing the reading for, was Sue's daughter and Bob's stepdaughter.

Bob was very adamant that I tell everyone that Sue had nothing to do with his murder, even though the police thought otherwise. Bob said that Sue was a very patient, gentle woman to have put up with him for so many years. At times, he said, the couple had 'agreed to disagree' — however, he wanted to point out that this never stopped them from loving each other.

During the reading I was given glimpses of different areas of Bob's life that I had to try and piece together. It was like a big jigsaw puzzle to understand who, what, where and why Bob Chappell was murdered.

- Bob showed me what a major achievement it was for him and Sue to have bought the yacht. He was disappointed that there had been some issues with it while it was being sailed down from Queensland. He was adamant that he was going to get everything sorted out before he and Sue went on a trip.
- He told me that poor Sue thought that he loved the yacht more than he loved her. He told me that the *Four Winds* was the love of his life.

- Bob said that the boat was on a new mooring. At first I thought that he meant it was anchored close to the yacht club. Sarah told me that it was moored in Sandy Bay, quite a distance from the yacht club. The only way to access the yacht was by dinghy.

- People had suggested that he should rename the yacht. Bob told me that he thought it was 'bad luck' to rename a yacht, so he left the name as it was. In hindsight, he said, maybe he should have renamed it because all it did was cause him bad luck and ultimately his death.

- Bob took me to his work. I could see that he worked at a hospital in Hobart and he was being pushed by other colleagues to retire. He showed me legal papers and I heard the word 'contracts'. He showed me that he had a project that he had been working on. He said that nobody was going to push him out until the project was completed. He worried that the person who was going to take over his position when he retired was too young and not intelligent enough to do the job. He showed me that he and the man had had words on many occasions.

- Bob felt that he was being forced into early retirement by some of the staff at the hospital and he was quite angry about that.

- I felt that someone wanted to silence him and I wondered if the disharmony at work was connected to Bob's murder.

I began to ask Bob to tell me what happened to him on the night he went missing. He showed me that he was working alone on the yacht because he wanted to trace an issue with the electrics. This was the first time that Bob had stayed on the yacht alone overnight. Bob was getting snappy about Sue getting in his way so she left. I could see that when Bob made up his mind to do something, there was no way that anyone could convince him to do otherwise. Bob showed the image of Sue going back to shore in the dinghy and then he went below deck to finish what he was doing.

Bob and his partner Sue were preparing the boat because they were planning to go on a trip with friends to Port Davey in the coming weeks and he wanted to make sure the yacht was in good working order.

When Bob disappeared, there had been a lot of people on or around the water during the day. I could hear splashing sounds and in the distance music and voices. I felt that there may have been people on shore having a party or barbecue to celebrate Australia Day. That night the wind had come up and I could hear ropes and metal parts of the yacht clanging in the breeze. Sarah confirmed to me that there were people having a party on shore not very far from where the *Four Winds* was moored.

Bob told me that because of the noise from the wind, at first he didn't realise that anybody had boarded his yacht. Bob said that he had been pretty busy looking at the wiring when he started to get tired. He sat down in the saloon area to have a rest and drifted off to sleep. He was woken up abruptly by a noise outside the cabin on the upper deck. He decided to go and see what it was. Initially he didn't see anything unusual so decided to go back down inside the cabin.

In my vision I could see that he was closely followed by a man dressed in black or dark-coloured clothes. Bob was on his way back down the stairs when he was hit from behind. I was shown the image of a man holding something up above his head, then hitting Bob on the back of the head. I question whether a knife was also used because I felt a very sharp shooting pain in my right shoulder blade. I could see that Bob was thrown down the stairs and fell face-first onto the floor of the saloon.

I can see Bob struggling to get up off the floor and he is engaged in a fight by the man. I then see the man pick up something cylindrical and bulky, which I later realised was one of the yacht's fire extinguishers. The man smashes Bob in the face with the extinguisher, breaking his jaw and knocking out some teeth. While doing the reading, I could feel the impact on his jaw in my own body. I watch as Bob falls lifelessly back to the floor, passing out from the impact. I am shown blood on the floor and on the steps of the cabin. I see that there were blood splatters on the wall from the blow to Bob's head.

I questioned if more than one person was aboard the boat at the time of Bob's death. I felt that there may have been more than one person involved.

Bob showed me a dark-coloured vehicle that was connected to the murderer parked in the carpark near the rowing sheds. He didn't give me that good a look at the car — all I could see was that it was a four-door sedan.

The next image I was shown was of Bob's body being wrapped in a sail or sail bag. The worst part of this image is that Bob told me that he was unconscious but still alive when he was wrapped up. I was shown the image of the yacht's winch and boom. I could see that ropes had been cut — some of them had become entangled, others were flapping loosely in the wind. Bob said that the winch ropes were wound around the winch the wrong way. Bob showed me that the missing ropes had been used to tie him up.

Bob showed me that they had used the boom and the winch to get his body off the boat by swinging the boom to the side and then lowering him into the water with the winch. Initially I couldn't work out if Bob's body had been taken somewhere else via a dinghy or whether it had been lowered into the water and then been caught under the yacht.

The one thing that Bob was persistent in telling me was that it was extremely important to get a copy of the tide charts. If he was caught up submerged under the boat, the tides and currents may be useful in determining where his remains were.

The biggest obstacle to finding Bob's remains was that it was two years since his disappearance. Because of how long he had been in the water and the sea life in the area, I felt that if his body was disposed of in the ocean, there would be little or no chance of finding or recovering it.

Bob kept showing me an area close to the sea that was not very built up. I could see a road that was close to the ocean and then he showed me an underwater view of eroded tree roots. I got the impression that he was trying to show me that his body may have been caught up in the roots or had been disposed of in an area like that. I was given the impression that his remains had been weighted down close to the treeline under the water. I was shown an image of chemicals floating to the surface — it looked like a chemical trail, like what you would see if oil or petrol is leaking in water.

The most frustrating thing about psychic detective work is that everything is shown in fragmented details. There are many pieces to the puzzle — and the hardest part is filling in the missing pieces and making a whole picture. I could feel that Bob was getting frustrated with me as he kept showing me the same information over and over again. Yet I just couldn't pinpoint the area he was talking about.

To try to determine what Bob was showing me, I printed out a map of the area where the boat was moored. I was drawn to two areas that fitted the image of the road running along the shore. The first location was Rosny and the second was Chinaman's Bay.

The map indicated how deep the water was and that the area between where the *Four Winds* was moored and Chinaman's Bay was very deep. After looking at the maps, I really thought it was a waste of time to try and find Bob's remains that way. White pointer sharks were known to frequent those waters and I felt that if his body had been disposed of there, it would be long gone.

Instead, I decided to focus on getting Bob to show me what type of people hung around the yacht club. I wanted him to show me if there was anyone unusual he had noticed around the time he had gone missing. He showed me that he was concerned about some people who hung around at the front of the rowing sheds close to where he and Sue would launch their dinghy. He told me that there were men who sat around drinking and smoking late at night and that at times he felt that he was being watched.

Bob showed me an image of himself parking the car in the carpark near the men. He then showed me an image of himself and Sue taking supplies onto the yacht, including bottles of wine and beer. Bob said he worried that someone would break into their car while he was on the yacht. Sarah confirmed to me that Bob was worried about the yacht being boarded and she said that on a couple of occasions things on the yacht had been moved.

I felt that there was some sort of drug connection to the yacht and asked Sarah if they had found any link to that. Sarah said her mother had worried about that too because the yacht had sailed around southeast Asia.

I asked Sarah if there was anything that went missing from the boat. Sarah said that the EPIRB went missing and was located by a local man. This made me wonder whether Bob would have had time to activate the EPIRB to try and alert someone that he was in trouble. From the vision I had of him being attacked on board the yacht, I wondered if that was possible.

Sarah said that the boat had been tampered with. Whoever had murdered Bob had tried to sink the yacht by cutting a hose in the toilet and by opening a seacock, or valve, under the flooring. The way the person/s had tried to sink the *Four Winds* indicated that they had limited knowledge about yachts. The seacock they opened and the hose they cut was not enough to sink the yacht swiftly — the *Four Winds* was discovered listing in the water on its mooring, with Bob nowhere to be found.

Sarah said that when her mother had left Bob on board and taken the dinghy back to shore, Sue had tied the dinghy to a ladder at the yacht club with three knots in her usual manner. Sarah said that a red waterproof jacket had been found on a brick wall outside a house in Margaret Street, a few blocks from the club. I tried to tune in to see how the jacket got there.

I asked Sarah if she knew anything about a letter. Bob kept showing me that he had received a letter of extortion. I felt that someone known to both Bob and Sue had sent him the letter asking for money. He told me that once he bought the yacht, this acquaintance had been keeping an eye on him and had told Bob he could afford to give him some money. I asked Sarah if there was any mention of a physical letter or an email demanding money from Bob. She wasn't aware of anything like that. Bob told me that he didn't tell anyone because he didn't want to bother Sue.

◎   ◎   ◎

All this new information also made me question if there were other lines of enquiry that should be looked at concerning Bob's disappearance. Were there drugs left on the *Four Winds* when Bob and Sue bought the boat? Did somebody board the yacht in search of drugs? Was there a case of extortion by a disgruntled acquaintance?

To be honest there were so many storylines that I was becoming confused by the information I was picking up. This case just kept getting bigger and bigger.

I asked Sarah were there any funds missing from the family's bank accounts. She said that at the time she was still in the process of trying to work everything out.

The one thing that I was certain of was that Bob Chappell was deceased, his body had not been found and an innocent woman had been sentenced to 26 years' gaol for his murder — later reduced to 23 years.

As the reading drew to a close, I felt the only way forward was to visit Tasmania to meet Sue Neill-Fraser and board the *Four Winds* to see if I could make sense of what I was picking up.

SEEKING FURTHER INFORMATION

Due to other engagements, I had to wait several months to visit Tasmania to continue investigating Bob's case. I flew to Hobart on 8 September 2011 to meet Eve and spend two days seeing if there was anything more that I could pick up about the case.

At Hobart Airport, Eve briefed me about the schedule for the whirlwind visit and introduced me to a very close friend of Sue's named Rebecca (Bec). It was great to meet Bec as she was able to fill in some of the missing parts of the enormous puzzle.

The day was grey and overcast. The wind was blowing and it was freezing. We caught a water taxi out to the *Four Winds* and I asked its skipper about the tides and currents in the vicinity of the yacht. He said that there were quite significant high and low tides in the area as well as very strong currents which would run across the bay towards Chinaman's Bay.

He told me that many things lost around the Royal Yacht Club would wash up around the coastal area of Tranmere. He said that there was a whole area on the other side of the bay where flotsam would wash up. I wondered if this could be where Bob's remains ended up. I guess we will never know.

The trip to the yacht took about 20 minutes. Once we arrived at The *Four Winds* I felt an overwhelming feeling of dread. The yacht felt like a 'ghost ship' — and I was to later find out that this was exactly what many of the locals called the yacht.

The yacht was in bad shape, with the entire deck covered in bird droppings and the paint starting to peel away in some areas. In all, the abandoned yacht was a pretty sad sight. I could feel Bob's disappointment at what had become of his beloved lady of the sea.

My main concern was whether the yacht would be able to speak to me and tell me what happened to him on that fateful night.

We opened the hatch and went down into the saloon. I was quite surprised at how big the yacht was. In its heyday it would have been amazing. Because of the attempted sinking, the objects in the *Four Winds* were in total disarray. There were life jackets, cushions, carpet tiles, bits of clothing and cooking utensils strewn all over the place. The boat had began to sink bow first, so most of the items on board were in the bow area.

The first thing I felt was an almighty hit to the side of my face — its impact was so hard I felt like my teeth had been knocked out of my jaw. I found it quite hard to speak at this point as the pain was so intense. Bob certainly did have a way of getting his message across to me.

I was then taken back in time while Bob showed me what else happened to him. He began by showing where the electrics were on the boat and what he was doing at the time he was attacked. He kept going on about his teeth being knocked out, so I tried to look around the cabin to see if I could find any sign of the missing teeth. The floor area had been pulled up as Bob had been tracing the wiring underneath it. I wondered if, with the water rushing into the cabin when the yacht had been scuttled, the teeth had been washed into a nook under the floor. Bob kept telling me that the missing tooth/teeth was under the boards near the bilge area. It was an overcast day and the power wasn't working on the yacht. Unfortunately, we did not have a torch with us and the light in the cabin was dim so it was impossible to do a thorough search. We decided to give up chasing that avenue.

Bob drew my attention to a wrench that he said was used to hit him on the head. I actually thought it quite odd that the wrench was still on the yacht and not taken off as evidence and fingerprinted. He also spoke about a gaff hook that he said was used to help to dispose of his body. Again, I wondered whether the gaff hook had been fingerprinted.

As I had boarded the yacht over two years after Bob's disappearance, I truly hoped that the wrench we found on the yacht was actually put there after the yacht had been searched. Perhaps the wrench had been left behind by tradesmen when work was done to re-float and keep the vessel intact.

During the trial, the prosecutor Tim Ellis surmised that Sue had murdered Bob with a wrench, but no wrench was produced as evidence. Ellis mentioned the wrench countless times during the trial. Bob's body was never found, so how could Tim Ellis be so sure that Sue used a wrench to murder Bob?

Ellis also speculated that following Bob's murder, Sue used latex gloves to clean up the crime. It came to light later at the appeal that the DNA in the latex glove that Ellis accused Sue of using to clean up the crime scene in fact came from Bob Chappell's son Tim, not Sue Neill-Fraser. How on earth could he be so wrong?

It was actually very beneficial to be on the boat and to pick up the energy of Bob and Sue there. As the day was quite windy, as it had been that Australia Day night, it was good to be able to listen to the sounds that Bob would have heard then. The clanging of the ropes and pulleys was quite loud even down in the saloon. The water lapping upon the side of the boat was also a significant sound. It made me question whether Bob would have heard the approach of a dinghy or anyone boarding his yacht.

I had wondered if Bob had worn boat shoes because he kept talking about his shoes. It was quite surreal to be on board the yacht. As soon as I had the thought Bob would say, it is over here or to go over there.

I wondered if he was wearing his glasses and he immediately showed me his glasses sitting on a cushion in the wheelhouse. I asked him what clothes he had on the night of his murder and he showed me he was wearing a white singlet. He then showed me an image of the 'Chesty Bonds man', which I felt meant he was wearing a Bonds brand singlet. I saw another image of him taking off his long-sleeved white shirt, which was lying near his glasses in the wheelhouse.

The shirt was stained with grease marks and sweat and there were also bloodstains on it, which I wondered if the police had checked for DNA. I realised that if the items I was shown were on board and were tested, they would not have been put back on the yacht. They should have been held by the police as evidence. I was really beginning to question if the police did investigate the case as well as they had claimed. The shirt was the same as the one Bob was wearing in a photograph that I used to tune in with — of him standing at the helm of the *Four Winds*. Surely the police would not have missed the shirt in the investigation of the boat.

Bob told me to go to the bow. He said that there was something in there I should look at. All the cushions had been pulled off the bunks and there were lots of discarded objects strewn throughout the cabin. I lifted up a cushion in the area Bob guided me to and found the needle part of a syringe in its plastic cover.

Was this item connected to the drugs that Sue thought could have been on board the yacht? Why hadn't the police taken it as evidence and tested it? Or did it get there more recently? There were also receipts for dive gear and an old envelope from a flower shop in Cairns with handwriting on it. These items seemed to have been connected to the previous owners and may have been important in understanding the history of the yacht. I was really beginning to understand the frustration that Bob and Sue felt about the investigation into his disappearance.

I was shown a vision of people coming onto the yacht when Bob and Sue weren't on board. The image was of some younger people. I could see that they would come and sleep on the boat overnight and help themselves to the supplies, especially the alcohol. I question if Bob or Sue had noticed that things had been taken or opened. As the boat was moored some distance offshore, I felt that the group could come and go as they pleased without people paying too much attention.

I could see a battered silver-grey sedan in a carpark that leads off Napoleon Street — around 52 Napoleon Street, Battery Point — just up the hill from Marieville Esplanade. I was shown a darker dinghy that could be used to access the *Four Winds* from the shoreline. I questioned if people would enter yachts and steal from them under the cover of darkness.

Bob seemed to be showing two different scenarios, and that was becoming confusing, just like when I was in my office and first tuned in to the case. I knew that there was a drug connection, that there had been intruders and that there had been a murder on board the yacht. The one thing I knew without a shadow of a doubt was that I didn't see Sue Neill-Fraser in any of these scenarios. Not once did I see her having a violent altercation with Bob. Yes, they may have had words, but isn't that what happens in most relationships? It was the intruders that had me stumped — who were they and why were they on board the yacht?

I went back into the main saloon and asked Bob to show me what happened. He told me that he had been tracing the electrical wiring when he decided to have a little rest. He showed me that he had poured himself a red wine and contemplated what his next move would be. Then he nodded off and lost track of what the time was.

He was woken by a noise on deck. At first he thought it was the wind, so he went up to take a look. He told me that

The cabin of the *Four Winds* after the yacht had been re-floated.
Source: Debbie Malone

The twin-masted *Four Winds.* Source: Debbie Malone

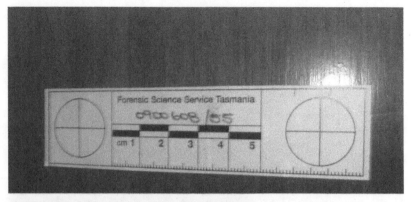

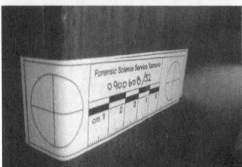

Images of forensic
markers on the yacht.
Source: Debbie Malone

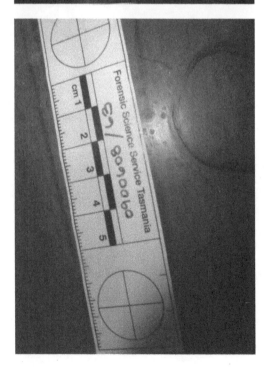

he could hear voices, but he wasn't sure if they came from a nearby yacht or from the shore. At first Bob didn't see anything and he turned around and headed back to the saloon. This is when he was struck from behind.

I felt that there was at least one person in the dinghy and one man on board the yacht, and that the intruders didn't realise that Bob was on board because the *Four Winds'* dinghy was not tied to the yacht. I felt the intruders were as surprised as Bob and that things got out of hand. The intruders panicked.

Bob showed me where the missing fire extinguisher was taken from — the bracket was still connected to the wall. He showed me where the lines had been cut and he wanted me to take note of the forensic markers and fingerprints that were marked throughout the cabin. I took photographs of the location for future reference.

I felt utter frustration as I was still being shown conflicting stories. There seemed to be a cross-over which was making it extremely hard to decipher the real truth behind Bob's disappearance.

No scenario I was shown included Sue. If Sue was the murderer, I am sure that I would have picked this up psychically. The fact that I didn't only confirmed to me that Sue was not Bob Chappell's killer.

I was shown the violent attack on Bob and I knew about his injuries. He wanted me to go on deck to have a look at the winch and ropes to see where they were cut and fouled. While I was standing on the deck, he pointed out the area where the dark-coloured car would park in the carpark off Napoleon Street. There was a business at the bottom of the carpark that Bob said knew a lot more than they were letting on. He said that the men who worked there had a direct view of the *Four Winds* and he said that we should visit them for a chat. I called Eve and pointed out the area that Bob was showing me in the carpark. We decided that when we went back to shore, we would go there and see if we could gather any more information.

Bob showed me how he was taken off the yacht using the boom and winch. I could see that the sails were all bunched up and there were ropes tangled everywhere. From the image I was being shown, it looked as if Bob had been put into a sail or sail bag and lowered down into the water.

I could then see the image of the sails in the water and an old inflatable dinghy beside the yacht. The dinghy was a dirty grey colour with scratches and marks on it. The most prominent thing Bob wanted to point out was that the dinghy did not belong to the *Four Winds*. He told me that he had just purchased a brand new dinghy which was white with three distinct blue stripes on either side.

The time on the yacht seemed to pass very quickly. There was so much information to digest and so many things to try and make sense of. I took my final photographs and then it was time to leave. There were so many mixed emotions that I picked up from the yacht — the feelings of sadness, despair, fear, anger, pain, broken dreams and, overwhelmingly, the feeling of the truth being hidden. This yacht was supposed to be the beginning of a new chapter in Bob and Sue's life, not the end for both of them.

Back on dry land in Hobart, we drove around to the yacht club and walked around. The distance from the boatshed to the yacht would be around 450 metres via dinghy. The view from the boatshed carpark would not be very clear at night. It gave me the feeling that it would have been quite easy for intruders to do whatever they pleased on any of the yachts under the cover of darkness. And the night Bob went missing, it was quite windy, which would have covered up the sounds of any commotion in the area.

Next we drove to the other carpark, the one off Napoleon Street that Bob had pointed out to me from the yacht. I couldn't believe what a perfect view could be obtained from here. Bob certainly knew what he was talking about when he guided me to this location. I walked around the carpark and then down to the business that he had pointed out. While I was walking along the road to the business, I was drawn to look at another business on the right. I couldn't believe what I was seeing. There were two red all-weather yachtsmen's jackets on display in a glass case — it was a similar type of jacket that had been found on the fence in Margaret Street. I got the feeling that this was a positive sign we were on the right track. How many businesses display products in this manner? It could not be a coincidence that the exact type of jacket had been found on the fence only metres down the road.

There was an antique shop called Annick's Antiques nearby. I felt very drawn to enter the shop and look at the antiques. I really didn't know why I was drawn into the shop, but because the feeling was so strong I decided to follow what I was being guided to do.

I absolutely love angels and when I entered I saw a little trinket box with a tiny cherub on top. The cherub was sitting down with a beautiful butterfly beneath him. Even though his tiny little wings were missing, I just had to buy it. While I was paying for the box, I began to make conversation with the shop owner. I asked her if she knew anything about the day the *Four Winds* sank?

She asked if I was talking about the 'ghost ship'. She said that everyone around here knew the yacht by that name. When I went on board earlier that day, the first words that I heard were 'the ghost ship'. I found it interesting that's what all the locals called the yacht. The woman said that when the *Four Winds* first sailed into Hobart everyone noticed it because it was the only double-masted yacht in the area. At the time it was thought that it was one of the most expensive yachts moored at the club.

She said her partner knew more about the boat than she did. He wasn't there at the time and she suggested we come back later to speak to him. She did know that one of the businesses down the driveway towards the waterfront had been involved in its salvage and re-floating.

I knew that I was drawn to the antique shop for a reason. I knew that Bob had been instrumental in leading me to this area.

I told Eve and the crew about the conversation. Eve went down to the maritime business to speak with them.

I had a really strong feeling that things were not as they seemed in this part of the waterfront. It seemed quite isolated and at night would be an excellent place from which to launch a dinghy and board the moored yachts without being sighted. While I was aboard the *Four Winds*, Bob was adamant that we investigate this area further. He made it very clear that this was the location from which he felt that he was being watched.

The view of the *Four Winds* was excellent, unhindered by obstacles, unlike the view from the boatshed carpark. The yacht was the largest one on the water and as it was double masted, there was no mistaking it.

If the *Four Winds* was under surveillance, as Bob and Sue had thought, then this was the place to be. I didn't feel very safe while I was there — it felt like a meeting place where business could be conducted unobserved. I questioned if this was where drug dealers would meet at night to do their deals. I wouldn't like to be there on my own at night.

Our next stop was to meet Sue's daughter Emma at Bob and Sue's home in Allison Street. The land between the yacht club and the residence was hilly and steep in parts. Arriving at the house was quite surreal. I could feel the years of love that had been shared with the family still evident. Yet there were such overwhelming feelings of sadness and anguish, now that the family had been shattered.

I went inside to have a cup of tea with Emma. She was living at the house with her daughter. Bob's energy was certainly still there because he was telling me to look around and was showing me where things were. Throughout the home were happy photographs of holidays and family celebrations. The love in the family was quite evident. Bob and Sue were in many of the photographs. I could see how much Bob loved his pipe — he was rarely without it in the photographs.

He led me out into the backyard and was adamant that I have a look at his tool shed. I felt that this was an area that he frequented in life as well as since his death.

When I asked Emma if they had found any letter extorting money, she said no. However, the police had confiscated Bob's computer so if anything had been sent as an email, then the police would have found it.

Visiting the yacht and the family home helped me greatly with my psychic impressions. I was now beginning to be able to put some more of the pieces together in this immense unsolved puzzle.

We stayed and chatted for a few hours, then it was time to head to the home of Sue's friend Bec, where we were staying the night. Bec and her partner were running a bed-and-breakfast.

Next morning, our first visit was to Risdon Prison where Sue Neill-Fraser was being held for Bob's murder. I really appreciated the opportunity to meet Sue. Bob had told me so much about her and the psychic impression I had picked up was that she was very determined, shy, quiet and family orientated.

I found it interesting that if Sue was supposedly the murderer of Bob Chappell, all the images I picked up about her were not of a murderer. Bob only showed me images of a woman whom he loved, challenged, shared his life with and, most of all, deeply respected. From what I could see, they were a typical couple who had their ups and downs. However, more than anything, I was shown the positives in their life. I questioned why, if the couple supposedly were having so many issues, they would even contemplate buying a yacht to sail during their retirement.

Prior to my visit to Tasmania, I had to apply for permission to visit Sue at the goal. I had to pass a number of security checks after the boom gate, the first being the visitors' reception area. The visitor number I was issued was scanned and a copy of my fingerprints was also scanned.

Once we were given clearance Eve and I were allowed entry into the gaol. After leaving the first clearance area we had to walk through to another entry point. There was a double-locked gate area that we had to pass through on our way to the prisoner visitors' centre. What was most interesting was the contrast of the surroundings. We were enclosed by razor wire and fencing, yet along the footpath leading to the centre there were beautiful beds of roses lining the footpath leading to the centre of the prison.

I began to hear the words from the theme song of the television show *Prisoner*: 'I used to give her roses, I wish I could again'. I thought how ironic the whole situation was. I felt that Bob was walking with Eve and me so that we could try and give Sue the strength she rightly deserved in order to fight the injustice that she had been served.

We were led into a small room with two tables and some chairs. Two other prisoners were already sitting with their visitors. A prison guard brought Sue into the room. She welcomed me with a big smile and shook my hand. I meet a lot of people in the type of work I do. First impressions are always correct when I assess a person. I looked at Sue and by shaking her hand I could feel her energy. I was definitely not in the presence of a cold-hearted murderer. I was in the presence of a gentle soul, who is kind and thoughtful.

I could sense her disbelief at her current situation. Bob and Sue should have been having the time of their lives, sailing around the world in their yacht. Sue should not be sitting in a gaol cell, she should not be without her beloved Bob.

Sue spoke about gaol life and about her hopes of an appeal. She said she had been treated quite well in Risdon.

She spent her days in the prison garden, as it gave her a peace and normality. Sue told me about the day of Bob's disappearance and her shock that the police didn't listen to her. It seemed from the onset that she was the one and only suspect in Bob's disappearance and murder. It was frustrating to hear Sue describe her ordeal.

Sue said that night was the first time that Bob had spent the night alone on the *Four Winds* and that he did not have a dinghy at the yacht in case he got into any trouble. Anyone watching the yacht would assume that if there was no dinghy tied to the yacht, there was no-one on board.

Sue told me about her mixing up the time and day she visited Bunnings. At the time she was interviewed by the police, she said, she thought that she had been at the store on Australia Day, the last day Bob was seen alive. In fact, on that night Sue received a phone call at 10.05 pm, which lasted for 29 minutes, from a stranger named Richard King. King said that Bob's younger daughter thought that something bad was going to happen to her father on the yacht. Sue was alarmed by the phone call from Richard King and was quite worried about Bob.

Sue said that she had had issues with memory loss and that when she was stressed she would get flustered and confused. The worst part about the whole ordeal, she said, was that she didn't even have time to mourn Bob because she was fighting to prove her innocence and truly find out what did happen to him. She talked about her concerns for her daughters and the issues that had arisen with Bob's children, who were trying to sell the yacht. Sue really wanted to keep the yacht because of the evidence it contained. All I could feel was pity for this beautiful strong woman.

View of Four Winds on the left hand side of frame from the Napoleon Street Carpark. Source: Debbie Malone

Even though Sue was under so much pressure, she was still very positive and hopeful about her future. I could see what a wonderful, strong woman she is and I was at a loss to see how the police could have treated her the way they did. It seemed to me that they were on a witch-hunt and Sue was their unlikely prey.

We talked about what had happened to the EPIRB and how it had been found washed up by a local man. Sue said that she had rung the mobile phone she had left with Bob at around 7 am on 27 January. Bob didn't answer the call.

Our visiting time passed by so quickly. An hour just wasn't long enough to ask all of the questions I needed to. I told Sue that I would do everything I could to find any other information about what had happened to Bob. I felt privileged to be able to meet Sue in person.

I was beginning to see what happened to Bob from two perspectives. I could see that he was quite a grumpy man who could be stuck in his ways and very difficult to deal with. However, this was not reason enough for Sue to have wanted to murder him.

I noticed that whenever Sue spoke about Bob, her eyes would light up and that she was always direct and open with all her answers about what happened — she wasn't trying to hide anything about the case. When someone doesn't speak to me directly or look me straight in the eye, I know they are hiding something. Sue came across to me as very honest and sincere.

Our next stop was the Royal Yacht Club of Tasmania where we had lunch. The yacht club is an interesting place and it was great to observe the types of people who were coming and going. There were two types: the old yachties and fishermen who were the salt of the earth — I could hear snippets of their conversations about their day sailing and their catches — and there were very well-dressed men and women who came in for a function. There were those with money and there were those who were doing it hard. I would have loved to speak to some of the old yachties because I am sure that they would have had their own opinions about what had happened to Bob.

Over lunch Eve and I discussed everything that I had picked up over the past two days. We talked about all the different scenarios I had seen and heard. The most obvious thing to me was that Sue Neill-Fraser was not Bob Chappell's killer. What I didn't know was how the police got it so wrong and I worried about how the verdict was going to be overturned.

Then it was time to head back to the airport for my flight to Sydney. My head was certainly swimming with information. I promised Eve I would keep in touch with any new information. Eve continued to work on the case, travelling to Hobart regularly over a four-year period to speak with Sue's family, friends, locals and witnesses to see if she could find any new clues about what happened to Bob Chappell.

* * *

On 6 March 2012, the Tasmanian Court of Criminal Appeal dismissed Sue's appeal against her conviction. The court did allow the appeal against sentence, which was reduced to 23 years from 20 August 2009 with eligibility for parole after Sue had served 13 years.

* * *

In May 2013 I met Eve at the premiere of her documentary *Shadow of Doubt* at the Chauvel Cinema in Sydney. Watching the film brought back the memories and visions I had seen while working on the case. Eve hoped that the documentary could help uncover new evidence that would prove Sue's innocence. On the night of the premiere I met Barbara Etter APM, a former Western Australian assistant commissioner of police, who has become involved in the case. Barbara is a truly amazing woman. Between Eve and Barbara, I think Sue has two very strong women on her side who have the ability to bring out the real truth behind the case.

THE HYPNOSIS SESSION

In October 2014 I suggested to Eve that I undergo hypnosis to see if I could be able to contact Bob Chappell. I have successfully made contact with victims in this way, so I thought this approach was worth trying. Eve did some research and decided that Alfred Podhorodecki, who is a forensic and clinical hypnotherapist and victimologist, was an appropriate practitioner to conduct the hypnosis.

I flew down to Melbourne on 22 November to do the session. We drove to Alfred's office in Mitcham. Alfred asked me to sit down in a reclining chair and he put a rug over me — when I go under hypnosis my temperature drops and I get very cold.

Before we started, Alfred asked a few questions and I told him that I had brought some of Bob's items to assist me in making contact. I said that Bob had a feeling of urgency and frustration about the situation that his family was in. Bob had also told me that he was a bit of a non-believer — I could feel a little scepticism from him about what I was about to go through, but as he was a physicist, his scepticism was totally expected.

Alfred asked me if I had felt Bob around me at other times and I explained that I had first met him in 2011. Through tuning in to his pipe and glasses, I was able to ascertain that he was deceased at our first meeting.

When Alfred asked what I wanted to achieve during the session, I said that I would like to work out what happened to Bob, see who the perpetrators were and what happened to his body. I wanted to be able to see if there were any descriptions of the perpetrators that I could bring forward. If possible, I wanted to know how many perpetrators there were.

I said that while under the hypnosis I wanted to hold a personal item of Bob's as I thought that it would give me a greater connection to him. Eve had given me an express post bag that Sarah had sent her. It contained a pipe. The smell was quite overwhelming and actually began to make me feel quite nauseous. However, Bob was extremely excited that he had his pipe back.

Alfred asked me to put on a pair of headphones. Gentle music was playing in the background and then he led me through a controlled meditation to hypnotise me. He guided me into a beautiful relaxing place.

Then he asked what I could see. I answered that I was standing on the bow of a ship. Alfred asked me to tell him about the ship. I told him that I'm very proud of this ship. It's a big achievement and I deserve it. People don't like the fact that I've got it.

Who was he speaking to? Alfred asked. Bob began to speak through me and he answered, 'It's Bob.'

Alfred told Bob that it was nice to speak with him. Did he smoke tobacco? Bob answered that he loved it.

Then Alfred asked Bob to tell him about the boat. Bob said that it was named the *Four Winds*. Alfred asked if that meant it had sails. Bob told him that it was a yacht and he was fixing it up because he was going on a trip. When asked what he remembered, Bob said that he had been putting a lot of effort into fixing up the yacht and that they were leaving after Australia Day.

As Bob was communicating through me, I got a really bad headache. Alfred asked Bob if it was my headache or was it to do with Bob. Bob said that the headache belonged to him. It happened while he was fixing up the boat. He said that those young louts had come on board again. Alfred asked Bob to focus on one person at a time.

The first person, who Bob called a lout, was aged around 17 to 25. Alfred asked Bob to tell him what he was wearing and describe his physical features. Bob said that he had seen the man before and that he used to hang around near the yacht club.

Is he the one who hit you? Alfred asked.

'Yes,' Bob said. 'He's been hanging round ... he used to bludge smokes off people. He's only scrawny. There were other people there to worry about when we drive the car down. Because I see they're going to break into the car. Sometimes they're just drinking out the front of the garage doors.

'They're hanging round near the dinghies — I feel like they're watching me. Sometimes I go out there and they are just hanging around in the dark, just sitting there smoking and drinking.'

Alfred said, 'Tell me, Bob, there was another person there — you said another male. Who's this other male?'

'I have seen him before,' Bob replied. 'I recognised his voice. Heard his voice. I heard the lout. I was working downstairs. I heard voices, but I thought they were going to pass the yacht. It didn't feel right because the *Four Winds* was further out than all the other boats. Didn't know why there was anybody out there, but it was Australia Day.'

When Alfred asked Bob what caused the headache, he replied, 'That lout hit me in the head.'

'What were you hit in the head with?'

'I dropped a wrench on the floor. I don't know if he hit me with a wrench or if it was a fire extinguisher. There was a big, big sound of metal on the ground once it hit me. It hit me in the jaw. I've lost some teeth.'

Then what happened? Alfred asked.

'It was cold, wet. Thrown overboard. I was there for so long. Nobody came. Then I had to come up — but then I had to leave my body.'

'You left?'

'Yes,' Bob replied. 'I wanted to know where Sue was. I was looking for Sue.'

'You love Sue?'

'I do, and the girls — I know they challenge me sometimes, but they're good girls.'

Alfred said, 'Tell me something. What time of the day or night did these people turn up on your yacht? What time?'

'I feel like about 9.30 at night,' Bob replied. 'I had some things to do. I just had a bee in my bonnet. Wanted to get it finished. Sue went off at me and told me to come home and to stop being stupid. Didn't want to come home, I wanted to get it fixed — I had a job to do. I like my own space. I don't like people talking in my ear all the time.'

'I just want you to hover over the boat as if your body's still there but your spirit's above it,' Alfred said. 'I'd like you to follow them — tell me the place where they started from, before they got to your boat.'

'It's a different dinghy to mine because the motor is different. Made a "putt putt" sound. Mine's better, mine's newer. It's different.'

'I'd like you to concentrate on that boat. I'd like you to go from the front to the starboard side and tell me the things you see. Any numbers or writing on it?'

'There're numbers on it. 19N. Looks like there's another one, but the last number's rubbed off. It's darker than mine. It's dirty.'

'Did anyone see them in the boat?'

'There was a party around from the yacht club — it sounded like the boat came from near where the carpark is. I thought they were going around to the party, but they stopped at me. If I'm at the bow of the yacht and I look to the left — five houses across, there's a little jetty coming out, a bit beaten up, with rocks around the bottom of it — and the party was coming from over there. They weren't invited to the party — they tried to gate-crash the party. They stole the dinghy.'

'Let's go back away from there, go back to the boat', Alfred said. 'In the boat, did they want something from you? Did they ask something from you?'

'Yes. They were telling me that they'd been sleeping there. They'd been sleeping on my yacht — I'd thought they were. I don't know what they were there for though. I think they thought they could just go and sleep there. I just had a little lamp down below the deck — it wasn't that bright. I think they thought there was no-one there. However, the other man came. There's two boats, two dinghies.

'Sometimes they'd have meetings in the carpark. I'd see a white car come down and I didn't realise who it was.'

Alfred asked, 'Did they remove anything from the boat other than you?'

'Oh yes. They put some weights around me. It was the fire extinguisher. They tried to lower me down. Something's gone wrong with my throat as well ... I feel like someone's got their hands on my throat. I feel tied up and my arms are hurting now. Feel like they broke my arm. They hurt my shoulder and my elbow.'

'I'd like you to go back to the boat,' Alfred said. 'Other than the fire extinguisher and some weights and ropes, horrible things, and you leaving the boat, did they take anything else?'

'I set off the EPIRB,' Bob said. 'I dropped it off the boat ... I heard someone coming. I heard noises so I quickly dropped it off the boat.'

'Was anything else taken?' Alfred asked. 'Where's this wrench, this wrench that was used to hurt you, where is it now?'

'I think it was thrown overboard.'

When Alfred asked if anything else was taken, Bob replied, 'No. I felt they were looking for something though — they made such a mess. They thought there was something there, but there wasn't. They were pulling up cushions. They were looking for money. I didn't have any. They went up to the bow.'

Alfred asked Bob to have a look at the hands of the people and describe what he could see. Bob replied, 'Callouses, cigarette burns, nicotine staining. I smell marijuana.'

Bob talked about a gold ring on the left hand. 'Not like a wedding ring, like a signet ring. I feel like he spins it around. It's got an insignia on it. It's not a horse, but like a horse-shoe or horse head but flat — it's like an achievement ring. He's got a gold watch on — he's quite showy. Feel like he could have a gold chain on his neck.'

At this point Alfred said, 'Whenever Debbie wants you to come back, you can come back. Time for you to rest now, Bob. We're all trying to help you. There's a lot of love here for you, Bob. When you go away, I want you to go away from here and Debbie will call you. Is that all right with you, Bob?

'On the count of five you're going to wake up and feel great. One, two, three — the whole body feels healthier — four, five — now fully awake.' As I open my eyes, he continued, 'It's important you drink some water and ground yourself. Putting your feet in the sea every now and then is always good. Thank you very much for the experience, Debbie. Anything you'd like to say?'

I said to Alfred, 'I just feel he doesn't want to go. I feel as if he's not ready to leave. It's like "you haven't got it, you haven't got it". I just don't know what it is.'

'Been long enough at it,' Alfred said. 'He's hearing me now through your subconscious mind and you'll wake up at that regular time, and he'll tell you that definitive thing that's going to help release that body. He needs to be released. It's not up to me to do that. I think you can do that, Debbie — you're empowered to do that. He's got unfinished business. He's not happy where he is, it needs to be resolved.'

I thanked Alfred for what he had done for me during the hypnosis. I said that I was feeling a bit woozy, nauseous, and that Bob is still attached to his body. While Alfred and I were talking, I noticed his ring, which, I tell him, is similar to the older man's ring that I saw through the hypnosis. The only difference is that Alfred's ring is silver and the other one is gold.

Alfred asked if the ring was like a Masonic ring and I agreed that it was. The older perpetrator had a nervous habit of spinning the ring around on his finger, which is something that stood out during the hypnosis session.

THE PHOTOGRAPHS

After I came out of the session, Eve asked if I would like to look at some photographs.

'Debbie, I have some printed pictures here,' Alfred said, 'and they have different people, different things, different events. Some of them may or may not have anything to do with the issue about Bob and his family, and what happened to Bob. What I'd like to do is show you a picture and you tell me what you see about that and who those people might be.'

Photo 1 was of the rowing shed carpark. I confirm that this is the location I was talking about. I show them where they would hang out. I point out an area in the photograph where they would sit and smoke. I also indicate where the grey dinghy comes from. I see that the perpetrators had tried to gate-crash a party through the back area and were told to go away, and then they stole the dinghy. People see them hanging around.

The next photograph was of a dinghy. I tell Alfred that this is the dinghy I was trying to describe.

When I was handed a picture of Sue, at first I feel happiness, then really sad — the photograph is of Sue on the *Four Winds*. The picture made me think of happier times and happier days.

The message I receive from Bob is that's when all our dreams were about to come true — this was a happy time, it's like all our hopes and dreams coming to fruition. Bob says, 'She's a beauty, you know, she's a beauty.' He's talking about both the yacht and Sue.

Alfred showed me another photograph and Bob says, 'Yeah, that was Sarah's wedding. They welcomed me with open arms even though I was a grumpy old bastard.'

The next photograph was of the boat on its mooring. Alfred asked me whether there was anything that was important about the photograph.

'Yep,' I replied. 'Let's see ... they didn't approach at the stern. They approached around the other side.' I drew an arrow on the picture to indicate the area. 'That's where they approached. Another one came around the back though. His dinghy was around the back. I can hear voices coming from two areas. The other thing is, I feel this is where the yacht was moored because they've approached from the stern here. The yacht club is back over there. Bob's telling me it's because of where the wind was — the *Four Winds* swung on the mooring. He's telling me he was lowered over on the other side. The sails were lowered down over there as well — I feel as though the ropes were cut.

Identikits of the three people I saw in my visions. Source: Debbie Malone

'He's showing me he was lowered down there and the dinghy was covered and they took that one. The other dinghy was set adrift. I feel they left in the darker dinghy and the *Four Winds* dinghy which is white was set adrift — nobody went to shore on that. The dinghy the perpetrators used is a dirty-looking thing. Bob is telling me he's very fussy and his dinghy has to be clean and tidy.

The next photograph was of bloodstains inside the *Four Winds* cabin. I get a headache as soon as I see it. I taste blood in my mouth and I can feel that my teeth have been knocked out. I get a pain in my head and I feel it's from a head injury. I get the feeling that there is something about the steering down underneath in the cabin area being missing. I wonder if the sextant is missing. Bob begins to show me something that they hit him with. It looks like a lever that could be off the steering. I see Bob and I can see that there's been a struggle in the cabin area. I feel someone else was injured besides Bob. I can see that someone is pulling Bob away by the leg — Bob tells me that it is the young guy.

Next I am shown a photograph of the cabin. I tell Alfred that this is the area that I see being ransacked. I also see that after they were knocked out, Bob's teeth may have fallen into the area where the floor had been lifted to trace the wires. I could see that there had been quite a struggle in the cabin. I see that when they put him into the water Bob wasn't dead. I feel like I am gurgling, like I am drowning. My hands and feet feel really tight like they are taped up and I feel as if Bob had been taped up. Bob shows me thick silver gaffer tape.

Bob begins to show me that he has a plastic bag on his head. I can feel that he has head injuries. He says that his arm is broken and that most of his injuries are on the right side of the head, the elbow and the arm. Bob says that he couldn't hit back because he's right-handed and his arm is already broken.

I am shown another photograph of the inside of the cabin. This time the picture is of the other side of the cabin. I can see the perpetrators rifling through things. Bob tells me that there are some tools missing from there, including a fire extinguisher. He shows me that there are two fire extinguishers — one is small, the other one is bigger and heavier — but only one of them is missing.

On the night he was murdered, he says, there was a pilot light on the yacht, but it wasn't fully lit and so the people thought it was okay to come on board.

The next photograph is of the cabin with the flooring all taken up. From this image, I get the message that there is unfinished business. Bob begins to talk about the tools. He is questioning whether some of the screwdrivers are missing and he also mentions a knife. Then Bob tells me that Sue is angry with him because he made such a mess. Bob says he started working on the yacht in one section and before fixing it he pulled up another area — he was trying to trace the wiring under the floor, but made a big mess trying to get to it.

The next picture is of some tape. Bob tells me that is the type of tape they used to secure his hands and feet. Bob shows me the image of a husky dog and a bear. I ask if these images are something to do with the brand of the tape. Bob says that the Bear brand is the one they used because it sticks the best. In the same image is a picture of Bob's glasses placed in the wheelhouse.

In all, Alfred and Eve showed me over 40 photographs, including pictures of Shane Barker and his house. The information connected to the Shane Barker case is in chapter 5.

◎ ◎ ◎

BACK IN TASMANIA

In March 2016 Eve and I discussed what the situation was with Sue's case and arranged to fly down to Hobart on 14 April for two days. We dropped off our gear at the hotel in Hobart and then paid a visit to the Royal Yacht Club carpark. By the time we arrived, the sun was already going down. I had never been there at that time of the day and it gave a completely different perspective on what it would have been like on the night that Bob Chappell went missing. Since my last visit the *Four Winds* had been sold and so was no longer at the mooring.

We stayed there until dark. The rowing club carpark area next to the Royal Yacht Club had a foreboding feeling at that time of night. It is dimly lit and personally I would not like to be there on my own at night. There were a number of cars parked there. A couple was sitting in their car and there were a few men fishing. The lighting of the area was quite subdued and the view out towards the area where the *Four Winds* had been moored was quite obscured.

I felt that at the time of Bob's murder it would have been quite hard to pinpoint exactly where the yacht was. Between the shore and where the *Four Winds* was moored were a number of other yachts, which would have obstructed the view from the shore.

I have checked to see how bright the moon was on the night of 26 January 2009 and the illumination was only 0.1%. On 14 April 2016, the evening we returned to the rowing shed carpark, the moon illumination was 52.1% and it was extremely dark — so it would have been much darker the night Bob was murdered. It makes you wonder how a witness could have seen a woman in a dinghy around midnight on 26 January 2009.

I asked Eve if it was possible to revisit the carpark off Napolean Street, Battery Point, because I also wanted to see what that area looked like at night. We drove around into the carpark and had a walk around the area. It was also very dark but there was a perfect view of the area where the *Four Winds* once moored. I truly felt that if the yacht had been watched, then the person watching would have been at this vantage point.

Eve and the crew stayed at the top of the carpark filming while I took a walk down to the roadway that leads to a maritime business. I felt extremely uneasy and that bad things had happened here, probably drug deals occurring at night. All the hairs on the back of my neck stood on end. The night was extremely still, when suddenly a very strong breeze engulfed me and froze me to the core. I just wanted to get the hell away from the area. I tried to calm myself down long enough to really tune in to the location. I felt that this area was where the dirty grey dinghy had been launched to go out to the *Four Winds*. No-one at the water's edge would have been able to see what was going on. You could board the yachts in the area without drawing attention to yourself.

My mind went back to 2011 and the first time I had visited the *Four Winds*. While I was on the yacht, Bob had insisted that this carpark off Napoleon Street and the surrounding shore area were of vital importance. I felt very strongly that the workers in the maritime business had a much greater knowledge of what had been going on in and around the waterfront area than they had ever let on to police.

◎   ◎   ◎

Eve had arranged for us to visit Sue at Risdon Prison before flying back to Sydney. It had been five years since I last met Sue. I was excited, yet I felt overwhelmingly sad because Sue was still in custody.

The morning of the visit everything seemed to be going wrong.

Our schedule was extremely tight and Risdon Prison is strict about visiting times. We just made it with a minute to spare. When you visit the gaol, you are given an identification number and your right hand is scanned. That morning my scan did not want to register. After re-doing the scan a number of times, I was finally given clearance to go through. The rose beds along the footpaths to the visitors' centre were in bloom and the ever-present fencing and razor wire was a firm reminder of where we were.

When we arrived at the centre we had to go through another scan point. First, my boots went off in the detector so I had to remove them and go through again, then my hand scan didn't work again. By this time I was getting quite nervous that something was going to stop me from visiting Sue.

Luckily everything worked out in the end and Eve and I were allowed into the small room to wait for Sue. Eve had told me that Sue's health had deteriorated significantly since my previous visit.

When Sue came into the room, she was in a wheelchair. She greeted us with her beautiful bright smile. For a woman under such duress and hardship, she still smiled. We talked about her current conditions and experiences. Sue said that issues with her feet were causing her extreme pain when she walked which had led to her being in the wheelchair. It was very distressing to see how much this had affected Sue's mobility.

Sue told me about the arrival of three new grandchildren and how sad she was to miss their births. Her mother had also passed.

Even though Sue had had some challenging experiences with her health and had missed important family events, she spoke very positively of her situation. She said that she had met some beautiful women while in prison, some of whom she helps with literacy, and by mentoring and writing their legal letters. Sue used to enjoy working in the prison garden because, she said, it helped her to retain her connection to the outside, but due to the problems with her feet she was now very restricted in what she could do.

Our one-hour visit was soon up. I was so pleased to have visited Sue. It only made me more determined to share her story by writing this chapter in my book.

On the way to the airport, we paid Sarah a visit and talked about her mother's case. I met Sue's two latest little grandchildren and felt guilty that I was free to meet them in their home whereas Sue was not.

◎　　◎　　◎

On 22 April 2016, just over a week after my visit to Hobart, Sue's legal team, headed by Tom Percy QC and Barbara Etter APM, made a landmark final appeal against Sue's conviction under new right-to-appeal legislation that was introduced in Tasmania in late 2015. Under the new laws, if a convicted person can satisfy the state's Court of Criminal Appeal that there is 'fresh and compelling evidence' and there has been a substantial miscarriage of justice, then the court may enter an order of acquittal or a retrial.

At the time of writing, Justice Shan Tennent had recused herself from the hearing (she was involved in an earlier appeal) and the new judge, Justice Brett, is scheduled to commence the case in May 2017.

◎　　◎　　◎

On a personal level, I do not feel that Sue Neill-Fraser is guilty of the murder of her partner Bob Chappell. While working on the case, I did not ever see any psychic evidence of Sue being involved in Bob's murder.

I have tuned in to items belonging to Bob Chappell and I have visited the *Four Winds* on its mooring. While I was on board, Bob showed me what happened on board the yacht that night. I clearly could see that there were intruders on the yacht and they have not been taken into account during the investigation of this case. I do know that people were accessing the yacht without Bob and Sue's permission.

I found a white shirt that had blood stains on it discarded on the seat area of the wheelhouse. The family identified the shirt as Bob's. Why was this clothing not tested for DNA or blood stains?

I met Sue Neill-Fraser on two occasions at Risdon Prison and I don't believe the woman I met was a murderer.

I have met Sue's daughters and visited the Chappell/Neill-Fraser family home. Sue's children and their family are a very loving, functional group of people who are devastated by the loss of Bob and the imprisonment of their mother Sue.

The whole case seems to have been very poorly investigated. The police seemed to have had their sights on only one suspect from the very start and that was Sue Neill-Fraser. It is such a shame that due to mismanagement of the investigation, the police have failed to arrest the real killer/s of Bob Chappell. The killers are still free while an innocent woman is locked up in prison for a crime she didn't commit.

To Sue, I hope that you finally receive the justice you so rightfully deserve. To Bob and Sue's families, I hope that the truth does come out. There has been enough pain and suffering for you all.

In all of this, there is one forgotten story and that is of Bob Chappell. Bob was a very gifted physicist who cared for his family and the community. He had a sense of adventure that he shared with his loving partner Sue. It is so sad that a dream they both shared of buying a yacht to sail in their retirement turned into the ultimate nightmare that would change both their lives forever.

◎　　◎　　◎

This whole case offers more questions than there are facts. This is one of the reasons that Eve Ash asked me to look into it to see if I could shed any light on what I saw as a psychic detective. To be honest, this is one of the most intriguing cases that I have worked on.

MARCH 23rd, 2017 – HYPNOSIS SESSION WITH ALFRED, COLIN McLAREN AND EVE ASH.

It was arranged that on 22 March I would fly to Melbourne and revisit Alfred Podhorodecki to once again go under hypnosis for the Bob Chappell and Sue Neill-Fraser case. The organisation that went into filming the hypnosis session, which was to take place the following day was quite complex. Eve had arranged for me to fly down from interstate, as well as having an amazing investigative expert, retired police detective sergeant and task force leader Colin McLaren, present at the session. Colin and I had met previously while working on the case of Mr Cruel in Victoria. Colin is now part of the investigative team working with Eve Ash on Bob Chappell's disappearance.

I hoped that I would be once again able to reconnect with Bob Chappell and I hoped that I would be able to finalise the identikits I needed to pass onto Colin.

I arrived in Melbourne and headed to Eve's place. By the time I got there, I was overwhelmed with excitement and dread about what the following day would bring. I was well aware that the day would be quite gruelling because I was going to undergo hypnosis to try and determine what the three suspects of interest would look like.

We awoke early the following morning as we had previously discussed that we would be leaving around 7.30 am from the city of Melbourne. It was approximately a 45-minute journey to Alfred's during peak hour. When we got there, the crew set up the camera and recording equipment to capture what happened during the session.

From the moment I arrived at Alfred's office I could feel the familiar presence of Bob. He was extremely impatient because he didn't want to wait for the crew to set up, he just wanted to tell his story as soon as possible.

The aim was for Alfred to put me under hypnosis and make contact with Bob Chappell. During the hypnosis session Alfred planned to speak with Bob and ask him to describe what happened to him on the night of his disappearance. Alfred was going to ask Bob to describe who he saw on the yacht with him that night and try and uncover how he was taken off the yacht and what happened to his body. Bob was also going to be asked to describe what the perpetrators looked like so I could draw their images to create identikits.

Colin McLaren arrived a short time later and it was time to begin the hypnosis session. Before being put under the hypnosis we agreed that Colin would also speak with Bob and ask him a number of questions pertaining to the case.

I sat in a reclining chair, lay back and listened to Alfred's instructions to put me under hypnosis. He led me through some breathing exercises and then through a meditation to take me into deep state of hypnotic relaxation.

Once I was in a deep hypnotic state I was able to make contact with Bob.

When Bob arrived I became the vessel for him to communicate through.

Alfred began to ask Bob if he was comfortable in meeting and speaking with Colin. After they were introduced Colin asked Bob what happened to him before and at the time of his death. Colin asked Bob to describe the people who were around him at the time of his death.

At times Bob was resistant to answering because there were questions that Bob told Colin that he didn't want to answer.

As Colin questioned him further, Bob relented and began to tell the truth about what really happened to him on the night of his murder.

While I was under hypnosis Colin showed Bob three different photoboards with photo images of eight different people. One board had photos of eight young females, another of eight young men, and the third board was of eight older men. All of the people in images pertaining to each age group were similar in nature. Colin then asked Bob to identify a female from the board, then a young male and then the older man.

When Bob identified the images he picked the right suspect on each photoboard, a 100% success rate. Colin was extremely happy with the result.

New Information that I picked up about the Bob Chappell case while under hypnosis:

- Bob and Sue knew the people who murdered Bob.
- There were three people connected to the murder of Bob Chappell.
- One of the vagrants was living in his car in the carpark at the rowing sheds. The car was a white vehicle.

- The owner of the vehicle is an older male who usually wears a peaked cap. He has a moustache, squinty blue-green eyes with a ruddy complexion. He looks like he is a drinker by the broken capillaries on his nose and face. This man had befriended Bob and Sue and at times would offer to help them to load and off-load supplies from their car to their dinghy and yacht. Bob and Sue had offered him bottles of alcohol as an exchange for assistance.
- Bob had had a few glasses of red wine on the night of the murder and had fallen asleep while intruders arrived at the boat.
- When they arrived Bob woke up in a disorientated state.
- The intruders intended to rob Bob. I saw that someone grabbed a wrench or hand tool and then hit Bob on the side of the face. The blow knocked him over. A struggle ensued and someone grabbed a fire extinguisher and hit Bob over the head. Bob fell lifelessly to the floor. During the attack Bob's teeth and jaw were smashed and some of his teeth were knocked out. The blood splatters on the walls occurred when Bob received from the blow from the fire extinguisher.
- At around the time the attack was taking place, a separate dinghy arrived at the yacht.
- Someone used gaffer tape to bind Bob's arms behind his back. They also bound his legs with the gaffer tape. They then find what looks like a sail or sail bag and wrap Bob up in it, using more gaffer tape to

secure him inside. Bob is still alive at this point. They then find some rope to tie Bob up further.

- They try to lift the hatches in the saloon and bow area of the yacht to get Bob's body up on the deck. The hatch seems to be stuck so the men try to drag Bob's body up the stairs.

- The next image I see is the cutting of ropes from the mast and tying them around Bob's wrapped-up body and then to the mast. The boom of the yacht is swung out so that Bob can be lowered into the water and tied to the side of the dinghy.

- At this stage Bob is unconscious and close to death. I feel that he drowns once he is lowered into the water.

- Before leaving the *Four Winds* the intruders intend to sink the yacht by cutting hoses under the floor and around the toilet.

- The intruders then motor along the Derwent in the dinghy and dispose of Bob's body in deep water towards the mouth of the Derwent River. Bob is weighted down with the fire extinguisher and the ropes are cut and he is set adrift.

- I see the sail/sail bag with Bob inside floating out to sea with the currents.

- The perpetrators are disappointed that when their return to shore the *Four Winds* has not yet sunk and is still above water.

After witnessing what happened to Bob through his own eyes during hypnosis, it was time to be brought out of the hypnosis session. Coming out from the hypnosis was extremely draining.

To be honest I was quite shocked by what I had just witnessed.

At no time during the hypnosis session did I ever see Sue Neill-Fraser on board the yacht while Bob was being attacked.

After returning to Sydney I redrew the identikits of the three people I saw on the yacht (using an app called Flashface). I was extremely happy with the end result. These images were as close to the images I saw under hypnosis as I could achieve with the limitations of the identikit software.

THE QUESTIONS

- What happened to Bob Chappell on 26 January 2009?
- Why was Sue Neill-Fraser charged with the murder of her partner Bob Chappell when there was no body and inconclusive circumstantial evidence?
- If there is no weapon, no forensic evidence linking Sue to the crime and no eye-witnesses, how can the jury be sure beyond reasonable doubt that Sue is guilty of Bob's murder?
- As Sue doesn't have any prior convictions, why was she a suspect?
- What was Sue's motive to kill her partner of 18 years?
- Why was the jury shown a picture of the *Four Winds* dinghy glowing with Luminol as if it was covered in blood, yet the confirmatory tests for blood were negative?
- Why did the court believe a man who had a criminal history about what he alleged occurred between Sue and himself?

- What did the man with the criminal history prove to gain if he testified against Sue Neill-Fraser?
- Why was a latex glove used as evidence of Sue cleaning up the crime, yet the DNA inside the glove was a match to Timothy Chappell (Bob's son), not Sue?
- Why was a blurred photo of a car that was 'similar' to the car Sue drove used to suggest that it was hers when the model, rego number or driver were not clearly identifiable?
- Why was the grey dinghy tied up to the *Four Winds* at 3.55 pm not investigated further?

This whole case gives you more questions than there are answers. It seems today there are still more questions than facts.

◎   ◎   ◎

It has been six years since I first met Eve Ash. Over that time Eve has diligently worked on the Bob Chappell case to uncover the truth. She continues to film, interview and explore leads that the police didn't ever look into. Eve's documentary Shadow of Doubt *has aired on the Crime and Investigation Network on Foxtel. The documentary is a fascinating insight into the case and the story behind it. Eve is the producer of* Undercurrent, *a TV series about the case.*

Chapter 4

The Disappearances of Dorothy Davis and Kerry Whelan

NAME: Dorothy Davis

MISSING SINCE: Friday, 30 May 1995

LAST SEEN: Lurline Bay, NSW

YEAR OF BIRTH: 1921

GENDER: Female

HEIGHT: 155 cm

BUILD: Medium

HAIR: Grey

EYES: Green

COMPLEXION: Fair

NAME: Kerry Whelan

MISSING SINCE: Friday, 6 May 1997

LAST SEEN: Parramatta, NSW

YEAR OF BIRTH: 1958

GENDER: Female

HEIGHT: Unknown

BUILD: Solid

HAIR: Dark brown-black

COMPLEXION: Medium

EYES: Hazel/brown

In 2011 I was involved in the second series of a television program called *The One* on Channel Seven. In each episode, we were set tasks to do in the studio as well as challenges that were filmed on location.

Each week one psychic was voted off the program until there were only three remaining. During the final episode, one psychic would be voted 'The One'. I made it through to the final, coming second.

The final on-location challenge was focused on the cold case of Kerry Whelan. It was hoped that the psychics would offer new information and perhaps evidence would come to light about what happened to Kerry the day she disappeared. It was also hoped that her remains would be located.

Before looking at Kerry's case, we need to look at an earlier mystery.

WHAT HAPPENED TO DOROTHY DAVIS?

Dorothy Ellen (Dottie) Davis, a 74-year-old grandmother, was last seen alive leaving her home at 9 Undine Street, Lurline Bay, in the eastern suburbs of Sydney, at around 1 pm on 30 May 1995.

On 1 November 2002, Bruce Allan Burrell was charged with Dorothy's murder. Burrell contested the charge but on 17 September 2007 a jury found him guilty.

Bruce Burrell was born on 25 January 1953 in the Goulburn area, where he was raised. Before September 1992 he worked as an executive in an advertising company called The Advertising Works in Sydney, and this is where he met his second wife Dallas Bromley, who was a graphic artist. One of the accounts Burrell was responsible for was Crown Equipment.

Bruce and Dallas married in 1985 and shortly afterwards they moved into a unit in Marine Parade, at Lurline Bay. Bernard and Kerry Whelan were guests at their wedding.

Dallas had grown up in Lurline Bay and had known Dorothy, who was a close friend of her parents, since she was a small child. In December 1984, Dorothy's husband died and left her with significant assets.

In 1988, Dallas and Bruce Burrell purchased a rural property of approximately 485 hectares in partnership with Dallas's parents, Les and Shirley Bromley. The property was called Hillydale and was adjacent to the Bungonia National Park near Marulan, in a remote area three hours' drive from Sydney.

In November 1993 Bruce approached the owner of a house on the corner of Wilson Street and Marine Parade, Lurline Bay, saying he would like to purchase the property, but at the time the owner was not interested. Several months later, in January 1994, Dallas was diagnosed with cancer and she began cancer treatment which continued until August.

By July Bruce Burrell had reached an agreement with the owner to buy the property at 34 Marine Parade for $600,000. He approached Dorothy Davis, asking to borrow $500,000 as a short-term loan in order to complete the purchase, explaining that Dallas really wanted the house. Dorothy agreed to lend him the money and wrote him a cheque on Friday, 8 July. The following Monday Dorothy's bank manager telephoned to let her know that the balance in her account was only $114,000. Dorothy instructed him to stop the cheque, explaining that the money was a short-term loan to a friend. On 12 August Dorothy wrote another cheque to Bruce Burrell, this time for $100,000.

Bruce deposited the money in his account the same day, telling his bank manager that the money was to be used as a deposit for a property near his current residence. On 20 August Burrell withdrew $90,000 in cash from his account.

Bruce didn't tell Dallas about his dealings with Dorothy until much later in the year, and then he altered the facts. He said that Dorothy had asked for his assistance and that she wished to conceal certain matters from her children (in fact, Dorothy told her daughter, Maree Dawes, about the two cheques). Further, he said that Dorothy gave him the money on condition that he repaid her in cash shortly after the sale went through and that, instead of the full $100,000, he would repay $90,000 and retain the remaining $10,000 in return for his assistance.

The contracts for the purchase of 34 Marine Parade were exchanged in August 1994 and the deposit paid. The purchase was completed in October. The money Dorothy lent Bruce was never used for the property. He took out a bank loan for the full purchase price.

By May 1995 Bruce had spent all the money Dorothy had lent him. In fact, he had been unemployed since 1992, had no regular source of income and was not receiving social security benefits. He was living off the income Dallas brought home from her fulltime job.

DOROTHY'S DISAPPEARANCE

Before Dorothy left her home on 30 May 1995 just after 1 pm, she had a brief conversation with a builder who was doing some work for her, telling him that she was going to walk around to see a friend, who was suffering from cancer and lived close by. Dorothy left meat defrosting on the kitchen bench, which indicated that she was expecting to return soon.

It is assumed that on the day Dorothy went missing, Bruce invited her to visit Dallas. As Dallas was at work and the only person home that day was Bruce, the invitation was a ploy to get her alone in the house so he could kill her.

Dorothy Davis suffered from a medical condition that made it painful for her to walk up hills. She walked down the hill from Undine Street to Marine Parade and then along the road to number 34. It is believed that Bruce had encouraged Dorothy to walk rather than to drive on the promise that he would give her a lift home — this also meant that he could avoid having to dispose of her car after he killed her.

An internal staircase at the Marine Parade house leads down from the kitchen/dining room area into the garage, which would have given Bruce the opportunity to move Dorothy's body from the property without being seen by his neighbours. Bruce Burrell was a tall, heavily built man who was 42 years old at the time. It would have been easy for him to move the body since Dorothy was of a slight build.

Sometime between 2.30 and 3.30 pm, Bruce Burrell left 34 Marine Parade in his four-wheel drive vehicle and drove to

Hillydale. He arrived around 5.30 pm that afternoon and left at approximately 7.45 pm, returning to his home in Lurline Bay that evening where he spent the night. The following morning he drove down to Hillydale again. It is not known exactly what time he left, but he returned to Sydney at about 2.30 pm, a six-hour round trip. It is believed that the reason Bruce undertook these two trips was to dispose of Dorothy Davis's body. To date Dorothy's remains have not been found.

By murdering Dorothy, Bruce Burrell would get rid of his $100,000 debt. Dorothy had began to pressure him to repay the loan and he was in no position to do so. Bruce Burrell was interviewed by police in late June 1995 in relation to Dorothy's disappearance, but his house and car were not examined until much later. When his home and car were searched, there was no forensic evidence found in either location.

THE KIDNAPPING AND MURDER OF KERRY WHELAN

Kerry Whelan was kidnapped on 6 May 1997 and killed a short time later. As with Dorothy Davis, her body has not been found. The common denominator in both women's disappearances is Bruce Burrell.

There are many similarities between the women's disappearances. Both women came from affluent families and Bruce Burrell had known them for many years. He had made contact with both women shortly before they disappeared, they were never seen alive after meeting him (although in Kerry's case that is presumed), he gave false details about his whereabouts at the times of both disappearances and he had the opportunity to dispose of the bodies at his property Hillydale.

⊚ ⊚ ⊚

Kerry was married to Bernard Whelan, a successful, wealthy businessman who was a senior executive at Crown Equipment, a large multinational company based in the United States which manufactures and sells fork-lifts. Bruce met Bernard when he handled the advertising account for Crown Equipment.

The Whelans lived on a 12-hectare property named Willow Park located at Kurrajong in the Blue Mountains, 80 kilometres northwest of Sydney. The couple had three children: Sarah, who was 15 at the time of her mother's disappearance, Matthew, then 13, and James, 11. Bernie had three children from his first marriage: Trevor, Shane and Marita.

In 1987, Bernard Whelan offered Bruce the job of advertising manager at Crown Equipment. While employed there, Bruce went to the Whelans' Kurrajong property on numerous occasions.

The Whelans often socialised with Bruce Burrell and they attended his 1985 wedding to his second wife Dallas. In December 1990 Bruce was made redundant and he was given the bad news by Bernard. After his departure from the company, the couples continued to keep in contact and catch up for social occasions. The two men were both interested in farming and sport shooting and were known to go away on shooting trips together.

During a trip in 1992, Bernard confided in Bruce that, because of the drought, he was experiencing difficulties with sustaining his cattle on his property. Bruce offered to agist the Whelans' prized cows, calves and bull, saying there was plenty of feed at Hillydale. Bernie arranged for the cattle to be transported to Hillydale. Only a few weeks after the cattle arrived, Bruce advised Bernie that a number of cattle had escaped into the Morton National Park. Mysteriously, all Bernie's pure-bred livestock were among the missing cattle.

Just 12 months later Bernie Whelan experienced another dubious episode involving Bruce. In 1993, Bruce called, asking if Bernie would consider selling his .44 magnum semi-automatic rifle to Burrell's neighbour who was having issues with feral pigs. Two weeks after Bruce took possession of the rifle, he rang Bernie to tell him the gun had been stolen from his car while he was at a sales meeting in Redfern. After this second incident, Bernie distanced himself from Bruce because he no longer trusted him.

Bruce had problems holding down a job — he didn't stay for very long in any position and was primarily living off the income his wife received from her job as a graphic artist. His relationship with Dallas began to deteriorate. Early in 1994, Dallas was diagnosed with cancer and was required to undergo chemotherapy. The same year Bruce purchased a green two-door Pajero 4WD and a Jaguar car. In 1995, Dallas started her own advertising business, which became very successful, and Bruce began to spend more and more time at the Hillydale property on his own.

In May 1996 Dallas decided it was time for the couple to separate. By December, they had reached a financial settlement which required each of them to borrow $125,000 so that they could pay out Dallas's parents for their share of Hillydale. Bruce ended up being the sole owner of the property and later lived there full time, although he was spending more than he was earning and found it difficult to make the mortgage payments. From July 1996 to May 1997 his sole income was from the sales of livestock, a motor vehicle and a tractor, plus a loan from his father.

On 21 May 1997, when Bruce Burrell was interviewed by police, he said that he had not received a wage for a number of years and that he had had to borrow money from his father to be able to survive financially for the previous six months. On 1 April that year his bank balance was $941.97 which was insufficient for him to pay the current month's loan repayment or any of his other regular living expenses.

In early 1997, Bruce had approached Peter Buckley, a friend and former work acquaintance who was a director of the company Ultratune, asking for a letter, which he could use to obtain a bank loan, saying that Bruce was employed by the firm. Buckley refused, so then Bruce sought to obtain money from Ultratune in return for assistance in a litigation case in Melbourne. Bruce was constantly on the phone to Peter Buckley asking for money, occasionally getting very pushy and once suggesting the two of them obtain a fraudulent bank loan. Buckley began to go to great lengths to avoid contact with him.

Bruce also had plans to buy property and set up a winery in Tasmania at this time and had asked a friend named Cathie Tulloh if she would move there with him. He was also planning improvements of over $60,000 to his cottage at Hillydale. Bruce Burrell was expecting a significant improvement in his financial situation.

◎   ◎   ◎

On 7 April 1997, Bruce made phone contact with Bernard Whelan, the first time they had spoken for at least four years. Bernard was surprised by the conversation — he expected that Bruce wanted a favour, but he did not ask for one. Indeed, the men just made general conversation about their families. Bernard told Bruce that he often flew to Adelaide for meetings on Wednesdays and that he also travelled interstate frequently for work.

The next time Bernard Whelan went to Adelaide was on 16 April. The same day Bruce Burrell made a surprise visit to the Whelans' home at Kurrajong. There he discovered that the front gate to the property was locked. He then drove to North Richmond, about 10 or so kilometres away, and called the Whelan house from a public phone box, despite having a mobile phone with him. The family's nanny and horse trainer Amanda Minton-Taylor answered the telephone. He introduced himself as an old friend of the family and was given the keypad security code so he could open the gate.

It is thought the reason Bruce used the public telephone rather than his traceable mobile was that he intended to kidnap Kerry Whelan that day, not realising that Amanda Minton-Taylor and the Whelans' 11-year-old son James were at home.

When he arrived at the house, Bruce was met by Kerry Whelan, who had a cup of coffee with him. Amanda was working outside and did not hear what they talked about. However, James Whelan said he overheard Bruce tell his mother that he had been to the pistol club in Lithgow. (This was found to be untrue.) As he was leaving, Amanda Minton-Taylor witnessed Bruce giving Kerry a kiss on the cheek. Kerry said to Amanda, 'Can you do me a favour? You never saw him here. Don't tell anybody. Give me a couple of weeks and I'll tell you why. ... Don't worry. I am not having an affair.'

When Bruce Burrell was interviewed by police, he said he had visited Kerry with the intention of getting her husband's help to obtain work. He denied that he had made any arrangement to meet her after his visit to Kurrajong.

On the afternoon of Tuesday, 6 May, three weeks after Bruce's surprise visit, the Whelans were planning to fly to Adelaide. Kerry was due to meet her husband at 3.45 pm at his office at Crown Equipment at Smithfield. Bernard Whelan left his home at around 8 am that morning and spent the rest of the day at his office.

Kerry had told her husband that she had an appointment in Parramatta with a beautician or skin specialist and was going to leave her car in the Parkroyal Hotel carpark. She had made the note '9.30 am' in her diary. This was quite unusual as she normally noted the details of any engagement. After Kerry's disappearance, police checked beauticians and skin specialists in the Parramatta area and failed to find any evidence of her appointment that day.

Kerry left her home and drove to her nanny's home at Glossodia, arriving at approximately 8.20 am, and spoke to Amanda and her mother Marjorie. Allegedly, she was wearing $50,000 worth of jewellery. She said that she had an appointment in Parramatta at 9.30 am and was going to go shopping afterwards. Kerry left the Minton-Taylor home at about 8.45 am and spoke to her husband on the phone while driving. She seemed to be in a happy mood and didn't show any sign of stress or anxiety.

She drove her car into the underground carpark at the Parkroyal Hotel in Phillip Street at around 9.35 am. The hotel carpark had a security system comprised of a number of black-and-white cameras. The cameras recorded images a few seconds long with breaks of about five seconds between sequential shots. Kerry's car was recorded entering via the ramp from Phillip Street. She was then filmed walking out of the carpark along the right-hand, or western, side of the same ramp into Phillip Street. These last recorded images of Kerry were taken at 9.38:03 am and 9.38:08 am. She was heading either straight across Phillip Street or she may have turned west. Kerry's image disappeared into the light while she was walking up the ramp.

Earlier that morning, at 9.01:24 am, a Pajero 4WD, similar to the one owned by Bruce Burrell, was seen passing the Parkroyal Hotel. It is believed that he was waiting at the kerb to pick up Kerry. There is no camera evidence of Kerry entering the Pajero but the fact that her image wasn't captured on the CCTV footage that covered the pathways away from the hotel could indicate that she did get into a vehicle at the time.

At 9.38:46 am, less than a minute after Kerry was seen exiting the carpark via the ramp, a camera recorded the image of a two-door, two-toned Pajero, like the one owned by Bruce Burrell, pulling out from the kerb lane just west of the ramp and then travelling in an easterly direction down Phillip Street.

At the time of Kerry's disappearance, police found that there were only 1716 two-door Pajeros of the relevant model sold throughout Australia between 1991 and 1997. The police contacted many of the owners of these vehicles but could not identify who was driving the car seen near the Parkroyal Hotel that day.

When Kerry failed to meet Bernard at his office that afternoon, he went searching for her and found her car still parked in the hotel carpark. At this point, he rang the police and they began searching for her.

RANSOM LETTER

On 7 May Bernard Whelan received a ransom letter through the mail to his home address. It read:

There will be no second chances. Follow all instructions or your wife will die.

By the time you receive this letter she will be safely in our keeping.

To ensure her safe return you must at no time bring in the police the press any authorities or outside assistance. We will know if you do so.

The consequences of breaching this rule will be dire for your wife.

You are not our first Australian target there have been others. You have not heard of this in the past because they have implicitly followed all instructions and been reunited with there loved ones.

Do not underestimate our capabilities.

We will know if you breach any conditions at any time and you and your family will not see her again. This is our only guarantee.

The ransom for her return is one million US dollars. The rate of exchange means you will pay one

million two hundred fifty thousand Australian dollars
to be paid in one hundred dollar Australian notes.
Ensure only the new plastic notes are used. No paper
currency. No consecutively numbered notes. The
money is to be delivered in a heavy duty green plastic
garbage bag.

The money is not to be photo copied. No remote
transmitting devices. No radio active dusts. No dyes.
No means of tracing the money is to be used.

We are able to scan and test for all such devices
and any other method you may use. Do not be tempted
for if anything is used to trace the money it will not be
collected and your wife will die. No further contact
will be made.

You have seven days. When the money is ready
you are to put an advertisement in the public notice
section of the Sydney Daily Telegraph newspaper
saying:

'Anyone who witnessed a white Volkswagon
beetle parked beside the eastern gates of the Sydney
Olympic site at 10.30 pm on Tuesday 8.4.97 please
call ... then put your home telephone number at the
end of the advertisement.

After the advertisement has been in the newspaper
we will be in contact within three days at your home
to tell you the next step. Be ready to leave with the
money at any time.

The money is to be delivered by you and nobody
else. Do not substitute yourself for the delivery. You
must be alone. Have no wires on yourself or in the car

you use. We will know if you try to use them. Do not use the car radio.

Any sign of outside involvement or interference and your wife will die.

We will be aware of everything you do. Take care this is your only means of ever seeing her alive again.

The ransom letter had been posted the previous day and it was processed via a mail centre in the Leighton Field area. This meant that the letter could have been posted in an area that covered Silverwater, Merrylands, Bankstown and Bargo.

The ransom letter was typed on a Canon typewriter, using a Canon Orator 10 daisy wheel. At the time of Kerry's disappearance Bruce Burrell owned a Canon QS 100 typewriter, although it could not be shown that the daisy wheel and the ribbon cartridge found in the typewriter were used to produce the ransom letter. It is thought that the letter was typed in April, at the time Bruce Burrell visited Kerry Whelan at Kurrajong and that he intended to abduct her then.

Bernard Whelan did place the advertisement in the *Daily Telegraph* from 13 to 20 May. Burrell was seen purchasing the newspaper on 13 May. The advertisement did not produce any response however.

On 23 May, Kathleen Pemberton, a part-time receptionist employed by Crown Equipment, received a phone call from a male at around 9.30 am, which she thought lasted less than a minute. The caller told her to tell Bernard Whelan that his wife Kerry was okay. She took some 'scattered notes' during the call and as soon as it was terminated contacted Bernard's assistant Mary Brady and then made more detailed notes while they were waiting for the police to arrive. The caller had told her that it was important that the police and media were to be called off. He also gave details that indicated he knew the contents of the ransom note.

The same day, the police began searching Bruce Burrell's property Hillydale. At 7.20 am, while police were at his property, Bruce slipped out of his house by a back route, drove his quad-bike over to his neighbour's property and borrowed his car. He drove the vehicle into Goulburn and was seen making a call from a public telephone booth at the front of the Empire Hotel at around 9.21 am, around the time Kathleen Pemberton received the call at Crown Equipment.

When Bruce Burrell was interviewed by the police on 15 June, he admitted being in Goulburn on 23 May and making two phone calls from public telephones, but denied either was to Crown Equipment.

ITEMS OF INTEREST FOUND AT HILLYDALE

Because of Bruce's unexpected visit to the Whelans' Kurrajong property three weeks before Kerry disappeared, he became the focus of the police investigation. The search of Hillydale lasted five days and involved a large number of police. The property is an extensive and remote natural wilderness surrounded by cliffs and it is littered with disused mine shafts. The police did not find any traces of Kerry Whelan.

Police examined Bruce's two vehicles — the green two-door Pajero 4WD and the Jaguar — for traces of any hair or of DNA that could be linked to Kerry. The Pajero was found to be dusty and its interior was dirty and contained a large number of hairs, but none of those analysed belonged to Kerry Whelan.

Two lists in Bruce's handwriting were found. At the murder trial, the Crown made the following interpretations of these lists (the Crown's suggested interpretations are in brackets).

The first list read:

- collection [*of the victim*]
- advertisement [*by Bernard Whelan of the kidnapping and ransom demand*]
- waiting [*while the money is obtained by Bernard Whelan*]
- how to proceed [*instructions for handing over the money*]
- pick up [*of the money*]
- cover all [*his tracks*]

The second list appeared to be notes for a ransom letter and had similarities with the letter sent to Bernard Whelan (again, the Crown's suggested interpretation are in brackets).

- has been K [*kidnapped*]
- no P [*no police*]
- letter within 2 days [*how to hand over the ransom*]
- nothing until received [*do nothing until the money is received*]
- stress '2' [*no police*]

Below is part of the ransom letter. The bracketed comments are once again the Crown's interpretation, in this case, linked to the lists above:

She will be safely in our keeping [collection; kidnapped]; you must at no time bring in the police the press any authorities or outside assistance [no police]; the ransom for her return is one million US dollars ... you have seven days [waiting]; then put the advertisement in the ... Telegraph ... we will be in contact within three days [letter within 2 days]; tell you the next step [how to proceed]; any sign of outside involvement ... and your wife will die [nothing until received; stress no police].

During the search of Hillydale, police found an almost empty bottle of chloroform locked in a gun cabinet in a walk-in wardrobe. Bruce Burrell had purchased the 200-millilitre bottle of chloroform one to three years earlier from a pharmacy at Maroubra, a Sydney suburb close to Lurline Bay, from where Dorothy Davis disappeared.

Two pages of a UBD street directory found in the Jaguar interested the police. The maps covered the area between Phillip Street in Parramatta and Crown Equipment's premises at Smithfield. The location of the Parkroyal Hotel was highlighted, as was the route from the hotel to the Crown Equipment offices in Smithfield. This led investigators to believe that Bruce Burrell had planned the route he would take once he had abducted Kerry Whelan.

Putting the pieces of evidence together, it could be surmised that Kerry expected to meet Bruce at the Parkroyal Hotel and got into his vehicle voluntarily, particularly since there was no report of any incidence between a man and woman in front of the hotel during the morning peak hour on an extremely busy street. Bruce may have been seeking Kerry's help, specifically by recommending that her husband re-employ him at Crown Equipment and by heading towards Bernard's office in Smithfield, he would have been reinforcing this idea. The Crown believed that Kerry was not immediately subdued on entering the car, but that Bruce drove to a quiet location somewhere between Phillip Street and Crown Equipment (there was a large open area highlighted in Burrell's street directory) and there used the chloroform to subdue her.

           ◈   ◈   ◈

Bruce Burrell had boasted on two occasions that it was possible to hide bodies near Hillydale. In December 1996, a woman named Jaqueline Pritchett visited his home and he pointed to the forest area beyond the property and said that it would be possible to hide a body out there and no-one would find it, and that he knew that area 'like the back of my hand'.

Earlier that same year he told Peter Buckley during a phone conversation that, 'You could get lost in that forest for weeks. You could bury a body out there no-one would find it.' He also said that the forest was full of mineshafts, dense scrub and cliffs.

The evidence strongly indicated that Kerry Whelan was dead. She had a close relationship with her husband and her three children and had no reason to disappear of her own volition. Kerry and Bernard had made plans for the future, including the trip to Adelaide and a holiday overseas. None of her bank accounts had been accessed since the day she disappeared. There were no records to suggest she left the country or any Medicare records that would support her seeking any medical attention since her disappearance.

All the evidence points to Bruce Burrell being guilty of kidnap and murder, including the circumstances of his visit to the Whelans, the CCTV evidence of the two-door Pajero near the Parkroyal Hotel, the lists found at Hillydale and the telephone calls he made on 23 May from Goulburn.

⚬ ⚬ ⚬

Although the bodies of Kerry Whelan and Dorothy Davis have not been found, Bruce Burrell was convicted of their murders. He was sentenced to life imprisonment plus 44 years for the murders. Burrell lost two appeals against his convictions in the New South Wales Court of Criminal Appeal and the High Court dismissed his application to appeal.

FILMING *THE ONE*

When we filmed the first part of the Kerry Whelan episode in *The One*, four psychics were left on the program. One of the contestants was voted off before we filmed part two on location at Hillydale. We were taken to the Parkroyal Hotel and then filmed separately. Each of us was taken into the Parkroyal carpark and given time to tune in to the location, then interviewed about our psychic impressions of what we felt had happened the day Kerry disappeared.

A few days later we were driven down to Goulburn and stayed overnight in a hotel. The following morning we were taken to Hillydale. It was the middle of winter and the temperature had fallen to around 0 degrees Celsius during the night. When we arrived at Hillydale there was frost all over the grass and it looked as if it had been snowing overnight. I remember how cold I felt that morning — my fingers and toes were numb. We were asked to stand in position around the dam on the property, while we were filmed for the opening of the episode. Then we were introduced to a retired police officer who had worked on the Whelan case and who explained what had taken place at Hillydale and the subsequent police search of the property.

After we were briefed about the case, we were filmed separately at the homestead. There, we were asked to tune in and try and make a psychic connection to what had happened to Kerry and then share our information on camera.

The way the house was positioned on the block was actually back to front — when you drove up from the road and along the driveway to the property, the first thing you could see was the back of the house. The front overlooked the dam and shearing sheds and the surrounding paddocks.

I was drawn to the back door area where I felt a connection to Bruce Burrell. I also felt drawn to the bathroom that was close to the back door. There was a bedroom near the back which had a clear view of the driveway leading up from the road. I felt that Burrell would look out the window to check if anyone was entering his property. I got a sense of uneasiness in that part of the house.

While I was being interviewed in the house, I was very drawn to the shearing shed. I wasn't really picking up a lot of information about Kerry Whelan. I was picking up another woman, Dorothy Davis.

When I told the producers that I was picking up Dorothy rather than Kerry, they became annoyed with me. They were not interested in Dorothy's disappearance — we were at the property to focus on Kerry Whelan and not Dorothy Davis, they said.

I said that when I work on murder cases, I couldn't control which victim came through to me the strongest, and that there must be a very good reason for Dorothy making her presence known. I find that if someone was a very strong and determined person when they were alive, then that is how they will present to me when they are in spirit. Dorothy may have been a frail little old lady, but she was still a very strong and forthright person who wanted her remains to be found.

However, the producers were not interested. Instead, I was ridiculed for not focusing on the task at hand. I was quite annoyed at the treatment that I received and found it hard to focus on what happened to Kerry. The whole time I was in the house, I could see and hear Dorothy telling me how important the shearing shed was. She kept telling me that Bruce Burrell would constantly look out the window of the living room, where I was being interviewed. She said that she was buried under the shed. Again I told the crew this and they just kept telling me to focus on Kerry Whelan.

The house was built up on a hill situated above a dam. The shearing shed was almost next to the dam. There were a number of fenced paddocks containing horses and to the right of the shearing shed was a large barn/stable area where vehicles and equipment were stored. None of the psychics was given access to this area, although I felt that it had some importance.

I felt that the remains of both women had not been taken inside the house itself, however they may have been brought onto the property by a four-wheel drive and that the vehicle may have been parked in or near the barn/stable after their disposal.

On each episode, before undertaking a challenge or a task, each psychic was put in 'lock-down' separately in order to tune in psychically to the task at hand. On this particular day, once each interview was completed in the house, we were locked in the shearing shed.

When I was put in lock-down, Dorothy would not leave me alone. I tried desperately to meditate and focus on what had happened to Kerry. However, Dorothy had other ideas. She told me that I didn't need to look any further because I was sitting above where her remains were. At one stage I asked the crew if I could walk outside and look around the shearing shed. The shed was raised above the ground and there were stairs that led up to it and a ramp down from the shed into a fenced-off area where the sheep would be kept after being shorn.

Underneath the shed was a poorly laid concrete slab. Due to erosion, a lot of the soil underneath the slab had been washed away, leaving gaping holes. I was given the strong impression that this is where Dorothy's remains were buried.

I described the psychic impressions I was receiving, only to be shut down by the crew again. By this point I was really getting annoyed and found it very difficult to focus on Kerry.

While I was sitting in the shed, the crew gave me a map of the surrounding bush area that was to be used when I undertook the psychic challenge. The distinctive things I was shown when I focused on it were pine trees, a dried-up riverbed and yellow sandy soil. I could see a dirt road leading down to the riverbed and that there was a town in the distance. The pine trees were planted in rows as in a pine forest and I could see that the sandy area was quite distinct from the other vegetation.

I received a very strong psychic impression that both the victims were killed before being taken to Hillydale. I felt that the women had been incapacitated and possibly drugged before they were killed.

While I was sitting in the shearing shed, I kept getting a strange sensation around my nose and mouth. It felt like my lips and nose were going numb — I wasn't sure if it was because the day was so cold, but it was more of a psychic feeling than a personal physical feeling. I could also detect a very strong chemical smell that wafted around me. The smell was similar to the smell at the dentist.

In the area where I was sitting, there were torn-up pieces of what could have been old white bedsheets. I was drawn to the rags and I wondered if Dorothy was trying to get my attention and tell me about something that had happened to her on the day she was murdered. I didn't feel that there was anything still in the shed that day that had anything do to with the murder, although I do think that Dorothy was trying to give me clues.

⊙ ⊙ ⊙

The psychic challenge was to be flown in a helicopter over the surrounding area in order to pinpoint a search area where

Kerry Whelan's remains might be found. In the helicopter I was asked to focus my psychic skills to where I wanted to search on the ground. GPS coordinates were taken while in the air, and when we landed, I was driven by four-wheel drive to my search area.

I had two problems to overcome at the start — one was my extreme fear of heights and the other was being terrified of travelling in a helicopter.

For each episode, we were given a specific outfit to wear during filming. That day I was wearing a long, hot pink woollen trench coat with matching hot pink leather gloves. I was so nervous that my hands sweated and the dye from the unlined gloves had come off onto my hands so they had become a hot pink. When I got into the helicopter, the pilot asked me to take off my gloves. However, the film crew told me to keep my gloves on to hide my hot pink hands. Two helicopters were involved in filming the challenge. A cameraman was with me in one helicopter. The second helicopter was there to record the GPS coordinates of the search area that I identified and to film where we flew to.

We passed over some pine trees which were planted on a flatter area than most of the land that we were flying over. I was really drawn to that area, particularly the left-hand side of the forest floor. As we flew in that direction I located a dried-up riverbed that had sandy yellow soil, which was what I had seen in my vision. There was also a dirt road that led to the area. I became quite excited because I felt that we were above the area of my visions.

Finally I felt that my time of tuning in wasn't wasted. I had located what I was looking for. When I found the spot I was asked to speak with the pilot of the second helicopter so that my GPS coordinates could be recorded. This was very important in order for me to complete the second part of the psychic challenge. To speak with the other pilot I had to push a button on the T-bar used for steering the helicopter. My pilot warned me that I needed to be quite gentle when I pushed the button. Unfortunately, because of the gloves I was wearing, I didn't realise that I had pushed it a bit too hard. Our helicopter lurched slightly sideways. The pilot instantly corrected our flight path, but the experience terrified me and I couldn't tune in to anything for a few moments. I just wanted to get the hell out of the helicopter and go home in one piece.

Unfortunately, the other helicopter pilot recorded the wrong GPS coordinates so that when we landed and I tried to locate the search area I'd identified, I was told it was out of the area the film crew was allowed to search. We didn't realise this until the driver of the four-wheel drive put the coordinates into his GPS and we ran out of road and came to the edge of the property. We tried a couple of different routes to get to the GPS point but each time we couldn't reach it. The driver said that my coordinates were over 30 kilometres away from where we were allowed to search. It was frustrating because when I was in the helicopter I was told I was well within the allowable search area and that it was possible to access the site by road. I was the last person to undertake the challenge that day and we were quickly running out of light.

I knew that what I had seen in my visions and what I had seen from the helicopter were the same and I desperately wanted to access the area in case it was the site where Kerry Whelan's remains were. Much to my disappointment, I was told that we

Helicopters in the paddock at Hillydale before the search for Kerry Whelan while filming 'The One'. Source: Debbie Malone

Satellite map of Hillydale. Source: Google Maps

couldn't search any further because of the error in writing down the GPS coordinates.

The whole day was very frustrating. After not being able to reach the search site, one of the producers wanted me to go on camera and say that I had made a mistake about the location. He wanted me to say that I couldn't tune in properly and so had to abandon my search of the property. I refused. My pilot confirmed that we had been in the allowable search area and that the coordinates had been recorded incorrectly — if I had made the mistake I was happy to admit it, but I was not willing to take the blame when it wasn't my fault. What I was most annoyed about was that no-one was listening to me about my experience with Dorothy Davis.

Kerry Whelan's remains were not located during the filming and the case wasn't investigated any further, which I found to be very frustrating. Dorothy followed me back to Sydney and was adamant that somehow or other I was going to help find out what happened to her.

When the episode aired, the Whelan family were extremely upset that Kerry's disappearance had been featured on the programme. According to media reports, Channel Seven had not contacted the family about the program, although I am not aware if this was the case. I felt greatly saddened that our attempts to assist with the case had caused the family any stress or duress.

FURTHER INVESTIGATIONS

A few months after the filming of *The One*, I was contacted by David Richardson from Channel Seven's *Today Tonight*, asking if I wanted to be involved in a segment for the program. David

Richardson is an incredible investigative journalist and I had worked with him and his crew on a number of occasions. I was happy to be working with them again. David asked me to meet him near a carpark on Marine Parade at Lurline Bay. He didn't give me any information about what the segment was about.

We met and I was driven a few blocks down the road to be interviewed in a house. It was on a corner and had a side entrance. Before we got out of the car, David asked me what my first impression of the house was.

The strong feeling I received was that of an older woman. I said to David that the woman's energy felt extremely familiar and I told him about my experience with Dorothy Davis and my visit to Hillydale. I told him that I had a strong feeling that someone had been murdered at the property. David told me to hold that thought until we entered the house.

David then explained that the story we were about to film was about the residual energy that can be left behind in homes when they are sold. He said that the current occupants had experienced many health problems and he wondered if I could help provide some answers about what energy, if any, was causing problems for them.

We entered the house and I was introduced to a familiar face. The current owner was Barbie Rogers, who had been one of the hosts of a program called *Great Temptation* that was very popular when I was young. We discussed the ongoing health problems that she and her husband had been suffering from. The couple had both consulted numerous doctors to try and find out what was wrong but had not found any answers.

We conducted the interview in the kitchen. David asked me what if anything I was picking up psychically.

I was suddenly transported back in time. I began to watch a man and an older woman having a heated argument in front of me. I saw the man grab the woman by the throat and begin to shake her. The man was large and much taller than the woman. He had blue eyes and a rounded face with light brown hair. His face was quite chubby and his cheeks were red with anger. His fat fingers were around the woman's throat. I can see the shocked look on the woman's face. She felt very familiar to me. I suddenly realised that the woman I was seeing was Dorothy Davis.

I saw the woman fall to the floor, then I saw the man place what looked to be a pair of stockings or pantyhose around her neck. He bent over and placed something over her nose and mouth, and that familiar dental smell I experienced at Hillydale appeared again. The man then dragged the woman down the stairs into the internal garage. I could hear thumps as she was dragged downstairs.

David asked me what I was seeing and I was suddenly thrust back into the here and now. I was quite shocked about what I had just experienced. David and Barbie told me then that the house is where Bruce Burrell lived at the time of Dorothy's disappearance.

I went down into the garage with the cameraman to see if I could pick up any further information. I could see that Dorothy's body had been taken down into the garage. Again, I was taken back in time and I could see her on the floor in front of me. I could see her lying on her side in a curled up position. Her frail little body looked lifeless to me. I didn't feel that Dorothy's remains were located on the property, although I did feel that Dorothy's spirit frequented the place. I felt very strongly that she wanted justice for what Bruce Burrell had done to her and her family.

Barbie told me that she had caught Bruce Burrell in her garage once. At the time she owned the same colour, make and model Jaguar as Bruce, and he had tried to access her vehicle. I found this to be quite disturbing and thought how lucky Barbie was to be safe from Burrell.

The rest of the interview is a blur as all I could focus on was what I witnessed Bruce Burrell doing to Dorothy in the kitchen and her lifeless body being dragged down into the garage.

I truly feel that Dorothy had orchestrated for me to be involved in the *Today Tonight* interview with David Richardson so that I was able to ascertain what really happened to her. The most frustrating part of this story is that to date I haven't been able to do anything with the information that I received psychically.

I did try to contact the producers of *The One* in order to get the address of Hillydale and I asked them if I could have a copy of the map that I tuned in to for the challenge because I felt that the locations I marked on it were important. I did try to organise production members from *The One* to contact one of the NSWPF Dog Unit officers who I have worked with, hoping that I could return to the property and do a further search. All avenues led to nothing.

I still wonder if Dorothy Davis's body is underneath the shearing shed. I know in my heart that Bruce Burrell did dispose of her remains at Hillydale, and I am sure the police believe that too. I just wonder if anyone has ever searched in, around or underneath the shearing shed.

During my entire time at Hillydale, Dorothy insisted on telling me that Bruce Burrell would look out of the living room window every day he lived there and she told me that he could see her and she could see him. He buried her close to his home because he felt confident that he would know if anyone came looking for her.

◉　　◉　　◉

Bernard Whelan died on 7 November 2015 without ever knowing what happened to his beloved wife Kerry. In his later years, he had developed dementia.

Bruce Burrell died at the Prince of Wales Hospital at Randwick, Sydney, from lung and liver cancer on 4 August 2016 aged 63 while still in prison custody. This despicable cold-hearted murderer went to the grave knowing where his victims' bodies were without ever telling the police or their families their locations. Bruce Burrell certainly has a lot to answer for — his greed and disrespect for others has affected so many people's lives. He never allowed any of the families the peace they so rightly deserve. This is a very tragic end for two beautiful families.

I hope that there will be a further search around the shearing shed and that one day the Davis and Whelan families will finally have closure. Both families deserve the right to lay their loved ones to rest and give them the burial they so rightly deserve.

Chapter 5

Who Shot Shane Barker?

NAME: Shane Barker

DATE OF BIRTH: 22 January 1973

DATE OF DEATH: 2 August 2009

AGE AT DEATH: 36

HEIGHT: 175–180 cm

BUILD: Medium

HAIR: Brown

EYES: Blue

COMPLEXION: Medium

Shane Barker.
Source: Paul Barker

Shane Barker was born on 22 January 1973 in Launceston, Tasmania. He was the second son of Rob and Barbara Barker. His brother Paul was four years older and his sister Nicole was four years younger.

For over 60 years the Barker family have lived in Campbell Town, a farming town in the northern midlands of Tasmania, with a population of around 800. Campbell Town is a popular tourist stop on the Midland Highway between Launceston and Hobart.

Shane, who was well known and liked by the locals, had worked as a postman, at the abattoir in Longford and then as a service station attendant. At the time of his death, Shane had been working in his dream job for just under two years — at Roberts Ltd. Roberts is a rural merchandise supplier that sells everything from farm and stock supplies to camping and fishing gear, as well as guns and ammunition.

An avid fishermen and hunter, Shane had been going on hunting trips since he was a boy. He was extremely close to his grandfather, who had taught him how to handle a weapon, and they had many adventures together.

In 2003 Shane married and the couple lived in a house in Campbell Town that Shane had owned before the marriage. They had a baby daughter in 2004; however, the marriage only lasted four years. When the couple divorced, they shared custody of their daughter. Shane treasured his little girl and always looked forward to the time he spent with her.

After the divorce Shane's Sunday night ritual was to visit his parents who lived 3 kilometres from his house. Shane's mother Barbara would do his washing and ironing and prepare her well-loved Sunday night roast dinner for the family.

On the night of 2 August 2009, Shane spent the evening with his parents as he always did. After they had dinner, his parents decided to watch *Dancing with the Stars* so Shane left their house at 7.10 pm to go home and watch the AFL. The weather that evening was very cold and windy and it was raining heavily.

When he got home, Shane did what he always did — he drove his car into the driveway, then left the engine running and the car lights on while he opened the garage door and the front door of the house, and then he parked the car in the garage.

On this particular night somebody was waiting in the darkness for Shane to arrive home.

At approximately 7.50 pm a good friend of Shane's rang him; however, the call went unanswered. This was unusual — Shane would always answer the phone or if he was busy he would call back as soon as he could. However, Shane never returned the call.

The following morning one of his workmates called Rob and Barbara to ask them why Shane hadn't turned up to work. This was also out of the ordinary — Shane was always very punctual. Although he started work at 8 am, he would arrive at 7.45 am and open up the premises.

Barbara thought that Shane may have slept in so she decided to go over to his house to check on him. When she arrived at his house, Shane's boss was already there. They knocked on the door and there was no answer. Barbara took out her phone and called Shane. The pair could hear his mobile ringing inside the house.

Just as Shane's father Rob arrived, Shane's boss found the house keys in the yard near the garage. When they tried to open the front door, it was dead-bolted from the inside. They decided that they should call the police.

The first police officer to arrive was also unable to get inside the house, so she grabbed a log of wood from the yard and smashed a window. The officer went inside with Barbara and Rob following closely behind her. They could see Shane's feet — his Blundstones boots and his jeans — and the officer immediately asked the family to wait outside so she could investigate further. Rob went into the hallway and saw his son lying on his back with blood trickling from his mouth. Shane had been shot several times at close range in the upper torso with a .22, a type of rifle many people in the farming community used to shoot rabbits and kangaroos.

To this day nobody has been charged with the murder of Shane Barker, the motive of the killer or killers is still a mystery and the murder weapon has not been found.

On the morning of the murder, a local man reportedly saw the driver of a white twin-cab ute talking to Shane outside his house at around 10.30 am. The witness said that the conversation became heated. A white dual-cab Toyota Hilux with a white canopy and Sunraysia wheels, produced between 1997 and 2005, was captured on CCTV footage driving along the main street of Campbell Town that morning. To date the vehicle and its driver have not been identified.

Initially, the family thought that Shane had had a heart attack. It wasn't until later that the family received the alarming news that Shane had been murdered. Paul Barker was at work in Launceston when his grandfather phoned to tell him his brother was dead. Paul's workmates drove him home and stayed with him until his brother-in-law Grant arrived. Grant is married to Paul and Shane's sister Nikki. Grant and Paul stopped to pick up Nikki, and then they drove to Shane's house to find out what had happened.

As they approached the house, they could see witches hats blocking off the road. Forensic officers were on the scene and a caravan had been set up. Police officers were wearing overalls and slippers, which indicated to them that Shane's death was definitely not a heart attack. There were at least 30 police officers in the front yard and ten police cars parked out the front. A uniformed officer tried to prevent Grant from driving any closer to the property. After talking to Senior Sergeant Rick Newman, they went over to their parents' home.

On investigation, it was surmised that the killer lay in wait for Shane and he was shot outside the house. It was thought that Shane managed to stumble inside and deadbolt the door. However, the gunshot wounds he had received were fatal. What baffled police the most is that Shane was a quiet, easygoing country boy who was well liked. Everybody in town knew Shane 'Bones' Barker and he could have been voted the town's favourite bloke. It was hard to understand why he was murdered. Lead investigator Inspector Scott Flude said, 'It was a targeted attack. Almost an assassination, I suppose you'd call it, and that's been the dilemma for us — finding a motive.'

The investigation team spent days at the crime scene scrutinising the area for evidence. Due to the torrential rain and wind on the night of the murder, the scene had been washed clean. Police have run checks on Toyota Hilux dual-cab vehicles with white canopies made between 1997 and 2005 but to date haven't located the vehicle seen in the CCTV footage.

⊚   ⊚   ⊚

I met Shane Barker in a very unconventional manner in November 2014. Firstly, when I met Shane he was already dead and, secondly, I met him while I was under hypnosis investigating another unsolved Tasmanian mystery. I was working with Eve Ash on the Bob Chappell–Sue Neill-Fraser case (see chapter 3) and underwent the hypnosis session to see if I could make contact with Bob Chappell, who had gone missing and was presumed murdered.

The hypnosis was at my suggestion as I had been successful previously making contact with victims this way. Alfred Podhorodecki, a forensic and clinical hypnotherapist and victimologist, put me under hypnosis and during the session I did make contact with Bob Chappell. At the end of the session Alfred showed me over 40 photographs mostly related to the case, but I was also shown a couple of unrelated photos — one of a house and the other of a man in his 30s with a goatie beard. The first impression I received was that something bad had happened to the man — I didn't learn he was Shane Barker until later — and that he was deceased. The first image that popped into my head was of guns. I felt that the man had been shot. He came across to me as a quiet person who had nice energy; however, I felt that there were people connected to him that were questionable. I saw an image of a motorbike and felt that there could be a 'bikie' connection. When I looked at the house in the photograph, a name came out of my mouth that shocked Eve because it matched a Crime Stoppers report about a person of interest in the Shane Barker murder.

I felt that the reason Shane was murdered was because he knew something about a cover-up. I could hear the words, 'wrong place, wrong time' and 'he knew too much'. I could see that there was a gun connection to the murder, but I was still trying to work out what it was.

After we finished the hypnosis session Eve and I arranged to meet up again to continue our work on the case.

CHANNELLING SHANE'S ENERGY

When I met Eve again in March 2016, we decided to contact the Barker family to see if they were open to me visiting them to try and bring out any new information concerning Shane's murder. The Barker family were very open to this offer.

The schedule for our trip was very tight. On 14 April I flew into Hobart and the next day we headed to Campbell Town. Our first stop was Roberts Ltd, the company in High Street where Shane was working at the time he was murdered. I was quite surprised that it did not look the way I thought a typical gun shop would look. Roberts is a local business that sells rural supplies, livestock, fishing and hunting goods, camping goods, guns and ammunition, sports and hunting apparel. The shop is quite large and it is divided off into different sections.

I walked around to see if I could psychically pick up any information, and on entering the area where the sporting/ outdoor leisure goods were sold I could immediately feel Shane's energy. I began to hear him talking to me as he guided me around the shop. He was very excited to show me the pink camouflage clothing and he told me that he had bought some for his little daughter. He then guided me to the area where the girls' clothing, western boots and gumboots were sold. I got the impression that Shane's daughter liked the colour pink because he kept guiding me to all of the pink items.

I asked him where the guns were and he took me over to a glass counter. When I looked into the case I could see boxes of ammunition, various types of hunting knives and high-powered torches. There wasn't a gun to be seen.

Shane then showed me the image of how the shop had changed since he had worked there. I could see a number of guns standing upright on a stand against the wall. The guns were all chained down and there was a glass case of ammunition similar to the one I was seeing in the shop in real time.

Shane showed me how proud he was to have worked in the shop. He said that it was his dream job and he was so sad that he was no longer part of it. He then guided me over to the office and made me pay attention to the computer on the desk. He told me that there was something very important on the computer which was related to why he was murdered.

I wished I could go into the office and look at the computer, or at least ask the man in the office some questions about it. Of course I could not, so I just had to be happy with what Shane was showing me. He told me that 'he knew too much'. He said that by accident he had found out something that related to ammunition. Shane gave me a psychic flash, showing me a print-out of an inventory of serial numbers. He made me look at the ammunition in the case again and then pay attention to the serial numbers on the boxes. He gave me the impression that there was a gap in the serial numbers and showed me that some of the boxes of ammunition had gone missing.

I am not sure if this was true, because I was only going by what Shane was showing me. However, he was really adamant that I keep looking at the computer and the ammunition. The other thing he wanted me to pay attention to was the camouflage clothing made by a brand called Ridgeline. The camouflage had very distinct patterns on it — I had never seen that type of print before. He said it was *important* that I remember the print. I was also shown an image of a deer's skull and antlers, which he said was another thing I needed to remember.

I felt that there was a definite connection to the shop and to what happened to Shane. He was telling me that part of the reason he was murdered was because he had found out something that he shouldn't have and someone didn't want him to spill the beans.

The next stop was to visit the Barker family residence.

As we were driving along the Midland Highway to the Barkers' property, Shane told me to take notice of the church and the cemetery. Near the church was a little opportunity shop close to the corner of the Midland Highway and William Street. I mentioned to Eve that there was something about this location that I was drawn to. I made a mental note of the feeling and then let the thought pass through my mind. It wasn't until later that night that I realised its importance.

The Barkers' home was just three kilometres away from St Luke's Church. I felt a strong feeling of dread as well as anticipation about meeting Shane's parents. I knew that Shane was with me and he wanted me to tell his family that he was now okay. He also showed me that he had an older man with him who I realised later to be his grandfather.

We were met by Rob and Barbara as well as a very boisterous cavoodle puppy called Theo belonging to Shane's sister Nikki. Shane's brother Paul works in Launceston and hadn't yet arrived. I was going to do a reading for the family, which was being filmed for the documentary.

From the moment I walked into the house I could see, feel and hear Shane's energy. He was very impatient about passing his messages on to his family. He kept telling me how excited he was to be back home and he was driving me crazy telling me to hurry up because he wanted to speak to his parents. The crew were filming an interview with his parents and I had to constantly remind him that he needed to wait until it was finished before I could pass on his messages.

At one stage Theo began to bark and, no matter what we did, he just wouldn't settle down. We tried everything to get him to stop but he had other plans. I could see Shane smiling at me with a big toothy grin and realised that he was the cause of Theo's barking. I asked Barbara if it was okay if I took Theo for a walk as I thought that would give the crew a chance to do the interview without being interrupted. Of course Theo absolutely loved me, as I am sure any dog does when they know that they are going for 'walkies'.

The moment I left the Barkers' house I could hear Shane talking to me loud and clear. I had never been to Campbell Town before and I felt that I was being guided along during our walk. The Barkers' property is off the highway and the end of their street leads onto farmland. I turned left as Shane was telling me to do. His energy was overwhelming and he was so excited that I was going to be his voice for now.

Shane told me to walk to the end of the street and then he showed me the images of himself and Paul as little boys — how the two of them would ride their bikes up and down the street and build ramps and jumps to ride over, how they would race each other from the top of the street to their home. Shane said that he was always the winner. I could see how close the boys were when they were younger and I could also see how competitive Shane was with Paul. He showed me how, even though Paul was the older, Shane had grown bigger than him. Shane gave me the impression that he was very cheeky and that he liked to stir up his brother to get a reaction.

Shane then showed me how he had a scar on the left side of his face under his eye. He said it was very important that I knew this. I told him to hold that thought because I wanted to remember everything for when I did the reading for his family. I walked around the block while Shane relayed stories of his childhood and the joy he had growing up in Campbell Town. Then he began to show me images of his beautiful little girl. When he spoke about his daughter, the love I could feel he had for her was overwhelming.

I walked the dog for around half an hour. It was extremely cold and the wind was like ice as the sun began to set. Theo was still unsettled when we arrived back at the house and kept barking and running around crazily. I could see that this was Shane's way of getting everyone's attention — he was ready to share his messages. Barbara and I went into the backyard and played with the dog to try and get him to settle down while the crew continued with their interviews. However, Theo had other ideas.

I got quite an uneasy feeling in the backyard. At the property boundary there was an open block of land. I got the feeling that someone had been watching the comings and goings of the Barkers at night prior to Shane's death. There was a very low perimeter fence and to be honest I really wanted to go inside the house as I didn't feel safe.

We stayed outside with the dog for around an hour and by this time it was getting really dark. Shane kept pacing back and forth, hassling me to tell his mum how ready he was to speak with her. I told Barbara how her beautiful boy was standing outside with us waiting very impatiently to make contact with the family. The hardest thing for me to deal with was that I was asked by the crew not to pass on any messages to Barbara until we were filming the interview so everything could be caught on camera.

As Barbara and I were almost numb from the cold, we decided that we had to go inside the house whether or not the crew had finished the interview. By this time Paul had arrived at the house. I was introduced to him and then it was arranged that Paul would go up the street and pick up pizzas for dinner.

Paul was extremely excited that we had come to Campbell Town to relook at his brother's murder. While he was waiting to get the pizzas, Paul decided to put a post on Facebook that we were at his family home to do an interview with the family. Well, this post really put a cat among the pigeons, as somebody took notice.

After we ate dinner, it was my turn to do a reading for the family. I was so grateful that I was finally able to share the messages from Shane with his family, as I didn't think he was going to be able to wait another minute.

Firstly, I asked the family if I could hold some personal items belonging to Shane and a photograph to tune in to. Paul placed a shoebox in front of me. It was filled with magazines, a cap, an engraved penknife, pen and other personal items. I was also given two plastic-tube type cases that each contained

This is the type of hat I saw in a vision connected to the shooting of Shane Barker.
Source: Shutterstock

a watch belonging to Shane. The family sat with me around the kitchen table full of anticipation. I hoped they wouldn't be disappointed by what was about to take place.

When I took the lid off the box I began to touch the items to see what, if any, had the most energy. There was a little metal tin that had Carlton football gambling chips in it. I heard a laugh from Shane that this was something that he had collected and was very fond of. There was a screwdriver inside the box with a yellow handle. Paul asked me what I picked up when I held it. I told him that I didn't get anything at all from it. I felt that Shane hadn't used it much or that it didn't belong to him. Paul had a cheeky look on his face but didn't say any more.

There was a penknife with engraving on it that Shane had received for his 21st birthday. However, the energy connected to the penknife wasn't very strong. I opened up the two watchcases and could feel a really strong connection by holding a silver watch that had a broken watchband. I shut my eyes for a moment and then Shane finally had his chance to speak with his family. Instantly I was given the image of Paul and Shane riding their bikes up and down the street that I had seen earlier when I walked the dog. I relayed this to Paul and could see an immediate change on his face.

He told me how he and Shane used to race each other from the top of the street to their house. Shane showed me how he was really competitive and how he always wanted to win. I suddenly understood why the dog was barking and why it was so important for me to take Theo for a walk up the street.

I asked the family about the scar that Shane showed me he had under his left eye. Everyone went silent, then they said that Shane didn't have a scar under his left eye. I could see Paul sitting and really thinking about what I had said. Then he looked at me in disbelief. 'I'll be buggered,' he said, 'how did you know that?' I said that Shane had shown me while I was on the walk. Paul said that when Shane was about seven, they were playing darts at their aunt and uncle's house and Shane had walked in front of the dartboard at the same time that Paul had thrown a dart and it hit him in the face. The dart had lodged just under Shane's left eye. As Paul told this story, the whole family remembered the scar. Paul just sat there in shock. He said that nobody would ever have known that unless I really was talking to Shane.

Shane certainly made his presence known during the reading. I could see him standing between Paul and Rob, and at times his cheeky sense of humour came through loud and clear. Shane said that I needed to remind Paul that even though he was the big brother, that Shane was actually the bigger brother in height. He showed me the two men standing side by side and I could see that there was a significant difference in their height. Shane smiled and said, 'and by the way I am the better looking of the two of us.' I pondered whether I should say this to Paul, when Shane said, 'Don't worry, he

Images of skull and antler I saw in a vision connected to Shane Barker's murder. Source: Shutterstock

will understand — just say it!' I passed on the message and the whole family began to laugh. They said that, yes, that was something Shane would say.

Shane then began to show me things about his life before his murder. He showed me the love he had for his grandfather and how the two of them went hunting when Shane was a boy. His grandfather had taught him to use a gun and had had a great influence on his life. Shane said that after his murder, his grandfather had lost the will to live and he had died of a broken heart. What was very special for me was to see that the pair had reunited in death.

He spoke about the remorse he had about the breakdown of his marriage and he said he had longed to have a wonderful family unit just like the one he had grown up in. His love for his parents and siblings was unquestionable.

Images of Shane playing with his little daughter began to appear in my mind. When I spoke to the family about the connection the two had, Barbara said that his daughter was the love of Shane's life. Shane told me how sad it was that since his death, his daughter didn't come to visit his parents much anymore.

While I was passing on these messages, Shane's grandfather, Rob's father, also appeared in the room with us all.

Shane showed me how, at the time of his murder, he was truly living the life. He told me that he absolutely loved his job and that he had a great group of friends. I asked Shane more about his life and he showed me that deer hunting was his real passion. I could see him dressed in camouflage clothing holding a rifle. On the living room wall there was a photograph of Shane with a huge deer that he had shot. Paul said that Shane had won the prize for shooting the biggest deer at a tournament on the mainland.

I began to see images of deer skulls and antlers floating before me. I asked the family about this and they told me that Shane had a large collection of skulls and antlers and that these had been left to his daughter. Shane showed me that people were jealous of the collection he had. He showed me that while he was on a hunting trip, another shooter in his party was jealous that Shane had shot the deer — the other man had thought it should have been his prize kill. Not knowing anything about guns or shooting, I didn't quite understand what the issue was. It wasn't until the family revealed how valuable the antlers are that I realised what Shane was trying to say. He showed me that the antlers were not in the family anymore, that after his death the antlers were sold as part of his estate and the proceeds were put into trust for Shane's daughter.

Barbara told me that she had always worried about Shane being a shooter and her concerns that something could happen to him with a gun. How extremely sad and ironic that her fears had came to pass — and that Shane died at the hands of a person with a gun.

I began to ask Shane what happened on the night of his murder. I could feel his energy combining with mine and I felt that he wanted me to channel what had happened to him. I don't normally allow this to happen unless I am under hypnosis. On this occasion I felt it was important for Shane to tell his story.

He showed me that he had been at his parents' house for dinner and then he drove home. He showed me that the night was cold, windy and wet. I saw him drive his car into the driveway. Shane said that this was what he always did. I could see that he left the car lights on so he could see to open the front door of his house.

After opening the door, he got back into the car and drove it into the garage. As he was walking back to the house, someone called out his name. The person was dressed in camouflage gear and was wearing either a dark-coloured cap or a balaclava. Shane showed me that he couldn't get a good look at the shooter's face because it was dark and the heavy rain was blurring his vision.

The man shot Shane several times in the upper torso. The first shots were not intended to kill, they were personal. The shooter wanted Shane to feel as much pain as possible. The next shot was closer to the heart but it wasn't enough to stop Shane in his tracks. Shane told me that the man had used a silencer on the rifle.

I was given the impression that there may have been two men on the night of the shooting. One was the main perpetrator, the other was there to witness what happened. It felt to me that the second man enjoyed what he saw. Both men had gun connections and I felt that they were hunters. I am still trying to work out if the shooter was a paid hit man and the other wanted to witness the killing or whether the shooter acted alone.

When I tuned in I saw a man near the garage area next to the fence and then I saw another man who was beside a caravan that was parked adjacent to the house on the boundary-fence line. I can't describe the second man — I just saw a dark silhouette. I noticed that there was a car parked halfway down East Street underneath a tree. I wondered if this was where the getaway car was parked.

Shane showed me that he managed to get himself inside his house — he was running on adrenalin and had enough energy left within him to be able to bolt the front door closed. He then attempted to get to the phone to call for help, but he collapsed in the hallway from the gunshot wounds and that is where he died. (Rob told me later that Shane's body was found on the hallway floor beneath the phone.)

Shane showed me that many things were going through his mind after he had been shot. He wondered why someone would do that to him. He worried about his daughter — about not being present in her life and about how her life would be if he didn't survive. He worried about what would happen to his parents and siblings. Shane also worried about his grandfather, who was one of his best friends.

Shane heard his mother's words in his head telling him that she worried about his safety, especially when it came to shooting. His mum had always worried that he might get shot. However, nobody ever thought that he would get shot like this. The fear was of him being on a hunting trip and being injured by a stray bullet.

While he lay there, he went over and over in his mind what had just taken place. The voice he had heard was familiar, and so were the clothes the man was wearing. The camouflage gear was one of the brands that he sold at Roberts. Shane tried to put a name to the voice but then it was too late. His heart was no longer beating.

He told me that after he realised that he was no longer alive, his whole perspective changed.

Shane began to show me an event that he had uncovered at work, which he didn't think was important at the time. When I visited Roberts I began to understand how important it was for me to visit his place of work to uncover new information. It also gave me an understanding of the layout of the office that helped me to understand the information that Shane wanted to share with me.

Shane began to give me images of walking into the office area and then he took me over to a computer. He showed me files that looked like an inventory of the ammunition and guns. He told me that when he was checking through the files, he found that some of the ammunition on the list was missing. He pointed out the numbers and then showed me that there was a gap in the numbers on the list, indicating that there were missing boxes of ammunition.

He said that he had spoken to someone in the company about the missing items but they were not worried and told Shane not to worry about it either. As Shane always did things by the rules, he wanted to look into the issue further, which made the other man get annoyed with him.

I feel that Shane uncovered that there was some kind of a cover-up and that someone was dealing the ammunition illegally. I believe that this could be connected to why Shane was shot. Shane kept telling me that he was in the wrong place at the wrong time. He was murdered because someone didn't want him to expose what they were doing.

I feel that the man who was working with Shane at the time of the discovery later left the company. I question if there is a connection to do with the man or men being hunters/shooters or whether they knew each other because of that. I felt there could be a connection between the murders of Bob Chappell and Shane Barker, which is to do with guns and ammunition.

Shane began to show me a vehicle. It wasn't the same as the one spotted on the CCTV footage. It was a white four-wheel drive with a flat — possibly checker-plate — tray at the back and fold-down sides. It had spotlights attached to the back of the cabin, like the ones used in spot-lighting and shooting. On the back window of the cabin is a sticker, which in my mind's eye was the logo of a longhorn or of deer antlers.

I saw a man wearing a cap that had flaps to cover his ears. The face wasn't clear in the vision. The hat reminded me of one that Kyle in *South Park* wore — I'm not sure what the connection was, but Shane seemed to think that it was important for me to make a note of it. Could the shooter have worn a hat like that or is it a suggestion that the person likes *South Park*?

I do need to point out that when I receive a vision, not everything I receive should be taken literally. The spirit world has a funny way of presenting images that may make sense to one person but seem like nonsense to others. It is important to understand that the images I have picked could be interpretations of what Shane was showing me. The image of the longhorns, for instance, is also a logo of RM Williams. Does the image mean that the person was known for wearing RM Williams clothing or is it simply that this sticker was on the back of the ute? I guess we will never know the answers about these images until the murderer is finally caught and brought to justice.

After relaying to his family the information that Shane thought was relevant, I could feel his energy withdrawing from my energy field. At this point, I usually feel very drained physically. On this occasion I was exhausted as I was suffering from a heavy case of the flu and Shane's energy was so strong that I had no choice whether I wanted to channel it or not.

Once our energies separated, the family asked me about people known to Shane who they thought may have been of interest to the case. As Shane and I were no longer connected psychically, when someone asked me a question, he communicated with me by speaking in my right ear.

A particular name would be said and Shane would instantly answer. His reaction, when he heard one particular name, was to show me the image of someone pointing their finger from the left side of the throat to the right side. For me this image indicates someone showing that they are going to die or are under threat.

A VISIT TO SHANE'S NEIGHBOURHOOD

The questions ceased and we decided to visit the cemetery where Shane was buried and also visit his house, where he was murdered. It was a cold, dark night. As we were driving along, I had visions of what I had seen during our drive from Roberts Ltd to the Barkers' home. I was made to look at the church and William Street, which I had been drawn to earlier in the day. Now I understood that it was Shane pointing out the cemetery where he was buried and the location of his house.

At the cemetery, once again I could hear Shane talk in my ear. The excitement I picked up from him was overwhelming. He was like a little boy who just couldn't wait any longer to be heard. While Eve and the film crew set up, Shane was bouncing around telling me to hurry up.

When I was waiting to begin filming, I spoke with Paul and Rob. Shane suddenly said that I needed to walk across five rows, turn right and then head to the back of the cemetery and I would find where he was laid to rest. We were in complete darkness and I hoped that I was hearing the right information. I told Rob and Paul what I was hearing and they looked at me in amazement. We will see what happens when we get there, Paul said. So I counted across five rows and then turned to the right and headed down to the back of the cemetery. Shane told me to walk across to the right and then stop. I was standing in front of Shane's plaque. Paul asked whether I had been there earlier that day. No, I told him, I had never been there before.

Even though I do what I do every day, the spirit world never ceases to amaze me. I pick up messages, yet I know that I am only the messenger. It is wonderful when I receive confirmation that I am picking up the correct information from the spirit world because sometimes I feel like I am playing a game of charades — meaning the images, signs and symbols I pick up don't always match what I am hearing and feeling.

It is only when all the pieces of the puzzle are put together that I am able to see the whole picture.

Standing in front of Shane's plaque, I couldn't help but feel overwhelming sadness. This murder was a waste of a young life. I saw visions of Shane's little girl. He showed me her coming to visit his grave. He showed me glimpses of his funeral and the people who came that day to pay their respects. He showed me how many people came to the funeral and the love and respect they had for him.

Shane's greatest wish from the spirit world was for his daughter to keep in contact with his family, and most importantly with his parents. To Rob and Barbara, she was their link to the son they had lost so tragically.

While I was speaking with Rob and Paul, I was drawn to a house just behind the cemetery. Rob and Paul told me that we were standing very close to the location of Shane's house. At that point I wondered why I was so sad about looking at the property. Shane told me that he had wanted the house to be for his daughter, but unfortunately it had been sold when his estate was settled.

I noticed the remnants of a little Carlton toy football figurine at the grave. It was missing a head and a leg. Paul said that Carlton was Shane's favourite team and that Paul's son had placed it there for his uncle. I also saw a little Christmas decoration that I felt very drawn to. Paul said that Shane's daughter had placed it there to celebrate Christmas with her daddy. She and a friend had also left a little pile of pinecones there. Paul told me that his niece and her friend would collect them and pretend they were camping under the pine trees.

While we were standing at the gravesite, I was told to turn and to look up towards the Midland Highway. I could see the headlights of a car parked on the other side of the road in front of the Campbell Town Community Health Service. The community centre wasn't open, yet the entire time we were at the cemetery the car stayed there with its headlights shining down towards us. At the time I thought that it was a little odd; however, it had been a long day and I had other things to focus on. Looking back, I realise that somebody must have seen Paul's Facebook post explaining what we were doing that night.

After we finished filming, we made arrangements with Paul to meet in the cemetery in the morning to have a better look at it and walk past Shane's house in the daylight.

I couldn't wait to go to bed. I was extremely tired and hadn't slept well the night before. However, Shane had other ideas. He kept me awake all night, filling my head with images of his life. At least I knew that he was keen to give me information to assist with his case.

Paul had posted on Facebook that we were going to be meeting at the cemetery at around 9 am that morning and that certainly did get the attention of a few people.

Paul was waiting for us when we arrived. The film crew set up all the gear and we did an interview about what we had experienced the night before. While we were talking, Paul said that he had been a sceptic about psychics, but after what he experienced last night he was now a believer. He told me that he had tested me when I was tuning in to the box of personal items that belonged to Shane. Paul had placed inside the box the yellow-handled screwdriver and a pen, which had nothing to do with Shane. He wanted to see if I was the 'real deal'. He apologised that he hadn't believed in me. I was really happy about his disclosure because it confirmed that I was on the right track.

The crew decided to walk down to Shane's house and film the outside of the property. They also filmed the view at the back of the church and the surrounding paddocks. While they were there, a guy from a house across the road yelled out at them and told them to leave the area. Nobody was trespassing or making any noise, or for that matter causing any issues, so it was quite interesting that the man became so irate.

Paul and I took a walk down to the house and past the front of the property. We were both on alert in case anything further was said. I wanted to see the house to get a better perspective on how the murderer/s entered the property, where he/they was waiting for Shane and how or where he/they left without being seen.

Shane's house was the only house on his side of East Street, down the hill from the cemetery and the church. It is a corner section, positioned on two large blocks of land, about five or six times larger than the other house blocks close by. It is adjoined by open paddocks with horses and next to this is War Memorial Oval. There are two other houses in East Street. One is at the junction of Truelands Road, next to a railway crossing. There is also a house directly across the road from Shane's with a train track between the house and the road. On the night of the murder the man who lives in the house opposite noticed that Shane's lights were on all night and he thought that Shane was having a big night. The neighbour didn't hear anything unusual that night; however, due to the bad weather the sounds may have been muffled. If the shooter had used a silencer on the rifle, like Shane had shown me, he wouldn't have heard the gunshots anyway.

East Street is a long street and there are only three properties on it. Shane's is the only property on his side of the street beside open paddocks with horses. The paddock adjoins War Memorial Oval. Directly across the road is his neighbour and then at the junction of Truelands Road and East Street is the other property, which is next to a railway crossing. Along East Street there are a couple of trees that have canopies, under which a car could park out of sight. There are no streetlights along the road, so if the murderer parked there he would not have been seen under the cover of the canopies and the darkness.

While we were standing in front of Shane's house, a metallic aqua-blue Toyota Corolla Seca, which was similar in shape to the 1998 hatchback, drove past us. The driver slowed the vehicle right down and took a really good look at Paul and me. The man was of a solid build, and he had blue eyes, a rounded face, big lips and big front teeth (buck teeth) and straight sandy brown hair, which was longer around the ears and reached down to his collar. He was wearing a red, white and blue short-sleeved checked shirt. I said to Paul that there was something suspicious about him and asked if he had ever seen the guy before. Paul said that he hadn't.

I decided not to worry about it and I tuned in to Shane's property for a few minutes to get my bearings about what happened that fateful night. I was really annoyed with myself that we hadn't visited the property at night as we had planned to do due to our time constraints.

Shane began to show me what happened. It was as though I was seeing things as if I had been with him at the time of his murder. I saw his car pull up in front of the garage, I saw him get out of the car and I saw the lights on. Then he opened the front door and returned to the car. Shane parked the car in the garage and was on his way back into the house. Someone called his name. He was startled that there was someone on the property.

Because of the darkness and the torrential rain, Shane wasn't able to see who the person was. The one thing that stood out though was that Shane recognised the voice. The man stood in the darkness dressed in camouflage gear. As Shane looked in the direction of the voice, he heard the familiar sound of a trigger clicking. He just stood there in disbelief. Psychically I heard one click and then two more in close succession. I saw Shane turn and run into his house clutching his stomach.

Then the vision faded and I was brought back to the present.

As I stood by the property, I was drawn to the shed that was on the right-hand side of the fenceline on East Street. I felt that possibly someone other than the shooter was also waiting for Shane and that this person wanted to witness Shane being shot.

Paul and I walked back to the cemetery to meet the others. While we had been away, someone had called the police, who were asking the film crew what was going on. As we had the full support of the family and nobody was breaking any laws, the police had left by the time Paul and I joined the crew.

While we were standing and chatting, we noticed that we were being watched by another man in a red ute, who was sitting in his car on the corner of William Street. At first we didn't pay much attention to him; however, he began to make it quite obvious that he was watching us. We took down his number plate and the description of the car, which was given to the police. The red ute had a red canopy on the back that had two windows on either side. He was wearing a black and red cap and a black and red shirt. He was aged in his late 20s to mid 30s and had dark, almost black hair, a stubbly beard and brown eyes. He was on the phone to someone for quite a while. I felt he was relaying what we were doing to someone else. When he noticed that we were looking at him, he put his head down to obscure his face. Again Paul didn't recognise the man.

When we drove away from the cemetery, we passed the man in the blue Toyota Corolla we had seen earlier parked on the side of the road in Pedder Street. He was on the phone and we all wondered if he was talking to the man in the red ute.

Shane Barker's cemetery plaque. Source: Debbie Malone

It was very interesting that so many people in the town were interested in what we were doing. These men may just have been 'rubber-neckers' or they may have had some interest in Shane's case.

When we left Campbell Town, the Barker family gave me one of Shane's watches to take home to tune in to further, and I have since managed to keep up the contact with Shane.

◎   ◎   ◎

Back in Sydney I did more research about Roberts Ltd, the firm Shane worked for. Shane had been employed by the manager of the time who had worked at the company for 20 years. In February 2008 the man was dismissed from Roberts and was convicted of stealing more than $26,000 from the company over a two-year period. He was sentenced in August 2010. I question if there was more to this story. I feel that Shane's death was connected to something that he found out unwittingly while he was at work. Was this the missing piece? Did Shane discover that the man was stealing the stock and did this have anything to do with his death?

I have talked to Paul on numerous occasions about the information that I have picked up from Shane, and Paul has spoken to police officers involved with the case about it. He gave me the phone number of one of the officers, who was interested in having a chat with me and I did speak with him briefly. He was going to contact me further but, as yet, has not called me back — and to be honest I don't think he will. I find it very frustrating that the police in Tasmania seek information from the public, yet when there is new information they don't follow it up.

I am open to waiting for the phone call from Tasmanian police. I just wonder how much longer the Barker family will have to wait to find out what really happened to their son, brother and loved one. It is so disappointing that some police officers are so closed-minded. They don't have to believe in psychics. All they have to do is to follow up on new leads and investigate them. Who knows — the information may lead them to something they haven't already investigated.

As for the two men in the vehicles in Campbell Town, the police have run checks on their number plates. As yet there is no news about what is their connection to the case. If there is one, I hope that the police will connect the dots.

My motto is: 'Psychics don't solve cases; however, their information can be utilised to provide new information.'

I hope the Barker family will one day find their peace and find out who killed Shane Barker and why he was so callously murdered. The truth is out there — only time will tell.

Chapter 6

P.S. I Love You: The Chris Noble Story

On 14 May 2015 I had the pleasure of meeting a beautiful woman named Elizabeth Noble. Elizabeth came to me for a reading to see if I could make contact with a loved one. At the time, I had no idea who Liz wished to contact or the reason why this person had transitioned into the spirit world. Within a few moments of tuning in to Liz, a very tragic story began to unfold.

◎   ◎   ◎

NAME: Chris Noble

DATE OF BIRTH: 7 March 1987

HEIGHT: 180 cm

BUILD: Muscular

HAIR: Brown, shaved

EYES: Brown

Chris Noble.
Source: Noble family

Chris Noble was just 27 years old when he and two of his neighbours were killed in a bomb blast that occurred in the convenience store below the apartments where they lived. The incident took place in Darling Street, Rozelle, Sydney in the early hours of Thursday, 4 September 2014. Adeel Khan, the store owner, who was also injured in the blast, has since been found guilty of three counts of manslaughter.

When I met Liz, Chris's mother, I could feel an overwhelming excitement of a young male energy entering the room with her. As soon as I tuned in to a T-shirt that belonged to Chris, I could hear and see him loud and clear. The first thing he wanted me to tell his mother was that he loved her and that he was alive and well in spirit. She was not to worry about how he had passed, as he knew that this was something that had been haunting her since the explosion.

Many images that made no sense to me at all began to flood into my head, but I knew that they were extremely important to Liz. I was shown the movie *P.S. I Love You.* I explained the film to Liz — it is a drama about a dead husband leaving messages for his widow, urging her to get on with her life — and she knew exactly what message her son was trying to send her.

Chris shared an apartment with two friends, Todd and Corey, above the 7–Eleven store run by Adeel Khan. Chris's neighbours lived in the flat next door with their baby son above a Vodafone store.

Chris and the other two victims were trapped by the fire that engulfed their apartments after Khan set off a bomb. The explosion took place at 4 am. Chris sent his mother a text message at 4.08 am. It said: 'I Love You!'

When I told Liz the words that Chris wanted me to pass onto her, she began to cry and she told me about the message Chris sent before he died. I could see him sitting beside his mum cuddling into her and trying to let her know from the other side that he was safe and well and that his love knew no boundaries.

Chris was very adamant that I explain to his mother that he had healed since the terrible ordeal. He showed me himself as the happy, cheeky, healthy young man that he was prior to his death. His cheeky smile lit up his entire face and there were no signs of the trauma that he experienced during his passing.

Chris then began to show me images of riding a pushbike. He showed me that he had been travelling in South America and had had the experience of a lifetime. He told me that after everything he had experienced during his travels — he did admit that at times he'd had a few close shaves along the way — he couldn't believe that he had made it back to Australia safely and then had his life cut short.

The hardest thing for Chris to accept was that he was supposedly home safe and sound, asleep in his own bed, and then he was involved in such a tragic end. Chris expressed his frustration at what had caused his death and the fact that there was nothing anybody could have done to save him. He showed me that after the explosion, Todd his flatmate had called out to him and tried to open Chris's door. Chris calmly said to Todd, 'I'm coming', so Todd let go of the door handle because he thought that he might be stopping Chris from being able to open the door. Todd headed towards the rear of the apartment, thinking that Chris was following him. When

Todd and Corey got out of the building, they realised Chris had not made it out so they tried to go back in after him.

It is thought that the floor and walls of Chris's room had been warped by the explosion, thus stopping the door from being able to be opened. There was a window in the room, but it had bars on it. Chris was trapped inside the building. If the security screens had not been blocking the windows, Chris would have been able to exit via the awning and leap to safety below.

Chris's feelings of desperation and frustration were extremely evident to me. However, I could also see the fact that he held no anger about what had happened to him. All I could feel was the love for Liz and his family emanating from him. Chris was just concerned about his family members left behind and the fact that he wanted them to know how much he loved and missed them. He did convey to me that it wasn't fair that he had to leave this earth so early because there were so many things he still wanted to do.

Chris's energy was so strong in the room, the way he was coming through as though he was still alive. It was now up to the family to start ticking some of Chris's wishes off their bucket list for him. Suddenly the image changed and I could see a group of people lining up to do a bike ride in his honour. When I passed this information onto Liz, she began to laugh and said that there had been talk of doing a bike ride in honour of Chris. The ride looked similar to a bike ride called a Tour for Cure to raise funds for people with cancer.

Liz explained that the family came from a small country town called Canowindra in the central west of New South Wales. Chris was very well known and liked in the town

Chris Noble wearing his
blue grid-iron football
jersey. Source: Noble family

and his loss was felt by all who knew him. The entire local
community has rallied around the family since Chris's passing
and it was very likely a ride for Chris would be organised in
his honour. Chris cheekily said that he hoped that his mother
could handle sitting on a bike for that long. He then winked
at me. Liz started to laugh. She said, 'That would be right —
that is something that Chris would say. Chris was always
cheeky like that.'

The images in my mind suddenly changed. Next Chris
showed me an image of himself standing proudly in a two-
tone football jersey, which was light blue and darker blue, and
another image of a mainly yellow jersey with blue on it. I saw
a wolf and wondered what this image related to — one of my

sons loves wolves and whenever I see this image I relate it to him, so I wasn't sure what this meant. The feeling of belonging became very strong to me with this image. However, the feeling of loss I felt at this time was overwhelming.

Liz is the mother of three adult children, Chris being the middle one. Being a mother myself, I could totally understand how hard it was for Liz and her husband to outlive one of their children. It is almost inconceivable to think that something so tragic could happen to innocent families like the Nobles and O'Briens in Australia.

Liz showed me a picture of Chris wearing a New South Wales grid-iron football jersey with the words 'Wolf Pack' and the number '52' on the front, and I realised that this was what Chris was trying to show me. Liz said that Chris was an aspiring grid-iron player who had a great connection to his team-mates. The wolf connection, the feeling of belonging and the name of his team suddenly began to make sense to me.

I suddenly saw many images of watches floating before my eyes, then Chris showed me a number of different watches. These floating watches were changing colour and shape and were various high-end brands. Then he showed the watches all proudly displayed side by side in a box.

The first line of a song started to play in my head: 'The lights go out and I can't be saved.'

Suddenly I was shown the image of an hourglass in which the sand was flowing very quickly through to the bottom. This is a familiar image I receive while doing readings. It indicates to me that the person has left this earth prematurely and they didn't get to fulfil their life's purpose. The image then reverted back to the watches and I could see them distorting and melting away. This was quite an unusual image but Chris said that it was important to let Liz know what I was seeing. Once again I relayed the image to Liz and her face lit up with a huge smile.

I could see numerous watches flashing by me. All the watches looked very expensive. Chris kept going on about a TAG Heuer that was very important to him. I am not sure if he had such a watch or whether it was one he had been saving for. The watch face was all black, its band and hands were black and the reverse of the watch was see-through, showing the mechanism. I had never seen a watch like this before. To be honest I had never really paid much attention to the TAG Heuer brand.

Liz told me that Chris was an avid watch collector and, yes, he did collect very expensive watches. For his birthday present, his brother and sister had bought him a special box to hold and display all his prized watches.

I got the strong impression that on Chris's recent trip to South America he had acquired a new watch that he had been saving for. Chris then showed me that all his watches were lost in the fire, and once again I saw the image of watches and time melting. This upset Chris the most because there was nothing of his precious belongings left for his family.

Liz agreed that after loosing Chris, one of the hardest things was that all his belongings were destroyed in the fire. So apart from losing her beautiful son Chris, she had very few mementos left behind as reminders of him.

Chris's mood then changed suddenly and I could see a newspaper with headlines about the fire. Chris pointed out a picture of himself and its caption which said he was in his

30s. He kept telling me that he was annoyed the journalist had got his age wrong and he was worried that he looked that old. He sat before me running his fingers over his shaved head and said cheekily that it must be because he was loosing his hair that people thought he was older than he really was. Liz and I laughed about his comments. Liz said that people did think Chris was older because of this. She told me to tell Chris not to worry as she had remedied the situation and the media had corrected his age when he passed to 27.

    ◉   ◉   ◉

After returning from conducting a day of readings, I felt that I was not alone. Chris followed me home and asked me to relay more messages to his mother.

That afternoon I needed to do some errands at the local shopping centre. Well, guess who came with me? As I walked through a newly opened part of the centre, I passed a TAG Heuer shop. I heard a male voice in my right ear telling me to look into the window display. I quickly recognised the voice and the cheeky energy to be no other than Chris Noble. He said, 'Wow, look at that watch, I really would have loved one like that!' The watch was the TAG Heuer Carrera Calibre 1887 Automatic Chronograph 45mm watch, costing $12,700. I couldn't believe what I was hearing. I smiled to myself and thought what a cheeky person Chris was, not to mention what a watch connoisseur he was.

Chris talked to me all afternoon. He kept saying that he didn't want to be forgotten. He repeatedly said to tell Liz not to forget about him. I decided to ring Liz and asked if it was okay if I included a chapter in this book about Chris and the experiences we had during the reading that afternoon. Liz was delighted and I can certainly confirm so was Chris.

I also passed on the description of the watch to Liz and she said that she had better start saving so that one day she could own a TAG Heuer watch in honour of her beautiful son Chris. After seeing how much the watch that Chris had pointed out to me was, I knew that Liz would be saving up for some time.

I explained to Liz that I was about to go away on holidays and I would be in contact with her on my return. Well, Chris had other ideas.

⊛ ⊛ ⊛

A few days later, my husband Warwick and I were due to fly to Europe for a month's holiday. The first place we visited was London. While there we did some tours on the Big Bus and it seemed that on every street corner there were signs advertising TAG Heuer watches. I knew that I would certainly not forget Mr Christopher Noble because he seemed to be giving me gentle reminders everywhere I went.

On the last leg of our trip we stopped over in Dubai. As we were walking through a busy shopping mall, a very familiar voice popped back into my head as we were about to pass a TAG Heuer shop. Loud and clear in my right ear I heard Chris's voice tell me about all of the amazing watches on display and that the watches in this particular shop were not even available in Australia. I just wanted to laugh to myself when I realised what was happening. Before meeting

Liz and Chris I would not have even noticed a TAG Heuer watch or noticed the shop. It seemed wherever I went , the TAG reminder was ever present and so was Chris Noble.

◎   ◎   ◎

When I returned home from my trip, I kept my promise to Liz and Chris to write about him — not only because I wanted to, but also because Chris is such a persistent and extremely special being who I could never let down. I started to write in between juggling readings for clients.

The hardest thing to comprehend was that Adeel Khan was very much aware of the people who lived above his shop. How could Khan, a father himself, even contemplate actions that could take the life of another. The fact was that this man knew that others lived above his shop and he still went ahead with bombing the building purely in pursuit of an insurance pay-out — in other words, for greed.

◎   ◎   ◎

As I write this Chris is showing me his family and those who were special in his life. Suddenly, the line of a song pops into my head: 'That *I love you* for what you are.'

These words are in memory of Chris's final words of love that he sent to his mother Liz in a text before he died.

Life is such a challenging thing. We don't always talk about our feelings and about what will happen to us when it is time to leave this earth. Death — yes, I did say the 'D' word: DEATH — is something we never wish to discuss or ever want to think about. It is inevitable that one day we all must die. It is the not knowing when or how that frightens most of us. I know many of us walk through life thinking death is only a word and that it will never affect us. Chris's message is a gentle reminder to us all that when we die, our love lives on from the other side and life does continue in the spirit world.

◎　　◎　　◎

While working on this chapter, I had a number of electrical issues that affected the internet and the computer. I am sure that cheeky Chris had a hand in the electronic interference. I needed to do some research about the case when the internet went down. I had left the room and was nowhere near the computer. Suddenly, my keyboard started to make a beeping noise and the sound got louder and louder. I came back to my office area and told Chris that I got the message that he wanted to tell me something. The screen on my computer then leapt into life and the webpage I was trying to access over four hours ago loaded. The beeping finally stopped.

I couldn't stop smiling because I knew who the cheeky computer gremlin controlling the internet was — it was cheeky Chris. I thanked him for making the internet finally work and I began to write more about this amazingly effervescent soul.

The song I had heard a few days earlier popped back into my head and I decided to look up all its lyrics. I felt that there was some message that Chris was trying to tell me by popping the song back into my head.

Again the computer started to beep and the cursor moved crazily on the screen. The curser moved rapidly through every word and then it suddenly stopped on the line, 'That I love you for what you are', and in the middle of the word 'love' — lo ve. I really felt that Chris wanted me to tell his mother how much he loved her. I immediately rang Liz and told her about my latest Chris experience. Liz sounded extremely tired when she answered the phone and Chris said that she needed to hear from him to cheer her up. I told Liz that I would email her the words of the song and this was her response:

> Deb,
> Thank you xx
> No doubt about you and Chris!
> Sorry if I was a bit vague this afternoon, was driving to Sydney and had become really tired and had pulled over and had a nap and had only woken up just prior to your phone call and was just regathering my wits as I had slept for an hour or so, must have been meant to be then. Love and care to you xx Liz

I have been working as a medium for 25 years and the most prominent message that I receive from both the living and the dead is of how much they wished they had said 'I love you' more to each other. So, from this day forward, remember to tell those you love that you love them so that you won't ever regret not saying it enough.

⊚ ⊚ ⊚

There were a few days when I was suffering with a migraine and hadn't been able to finish this chapter. I decided to go for a walk at Cronulla to clear my head so I could concentrate and write again. Just before I left the house I went back down to my computer and once again cheeky Chris wanted to let me know how impatient he was about me not finishing writing about him.

I wasn't touching the keyboard — in fact I was nowhere near the computer — and again it started beeping continuously. A vision of Chris and his cheeky face flashed into my mind. I told him that I would keep writing when I returned home. Then I drove down to the beach with my husband to take a refreshing walk. We decided to have lunch in Cronulla before returning home. There was music playing softly in the café. Suddenly I could hear the song I had been hearing connected to Chris. We are not alone, I said to my husband, Chris Noble has followed us and is playing his song to remind me to finish his chapter.

Warwick shook his head. 'I just can't take you anywhere without you having people in spirit around you,' he said. I totally agreed, but also felt how blessed I was to be able to communicate with spirit and share their messages with the living.

A few days later I was in the queue at the local post office and all at once I could feel the energy around me changing. A familiar voice popped into my head. Yes, it was Chris again, and he was telling me to look at the DVDs on the display next to where I was standing. They were copies of the movie called *P.S. I Love You.* I took a photograph of the DVDs and texted it to Liz, explaining that Chris wanted me to send her another message.

◎   ◎   ◎

On 5 August 2016, Adeel Ahmad Khan was sentenced in the New South Wales Supreme Court to a maximum of 40 years for the murder of Chris Noble, 27, the manslaughter of Bianka O'Brien, 31, and her one-year-old baby son Jude, for causing grievous bodily harm to Chris's flatmate Todd Fisher, wounding his second flatmate Corey Cameron and for destroying the building for financial gain. Khan will not be eligible for parole until 22 September 2044.

To this day, Khan refuses to admit that he set fire to his Rozelle shop, causing the fatal explosion. In debt to the amount of $373,000, he was only nine months into a five-year lease and intended to claim a $225,000 insurance payout. Khan showed no emotions at his sentencing. It was shocking to think that he had set up a network of ten petrol containers throughout the store connected by strips of petrol-soaked material and then set them all on fire knowing full well that people were asleep above and neighbouring his store.

Throughout the trial, Khan maintained his fake story that he was set upon by three armed robbers who tied him up for over five hours before they set his shop alight. What he didn't realise was that there was CCTV footage of him filling up containers with 38 litres of petrol at a service station two days before the fire. Thankfully that put an end to Khan's lies. I am so happy that he was sentenced for the crimes he committed.

Three young lives were lost due to Khan's greed and stupidity. I feel that at least in this case justice was done and the right person was held accountable.

◉　◎　◎

To the Noble family, Chris thanks you for keeping up the fight and ensuring that justice was done. He will always be by your side even from the spirit world.

To beautiful Elizabeth Noble, Chris has thrown down the gauntlet. It is your time to get fit, Mum, as we have some serious bike riding to do.

For the rest of the Noble family, Chris is very aware of his beautiful nephew and will certainly be letting you know when Uncle Chris is around. (And if he picks up any of Chris's cheeky habits, Chris has nothing to do with it.)

As I write these final words, the lights in my room are flickering on and off. I know that I am not alone and, yes, I know I am in the presence of a beautiful cheeky young man named Chris Noble. As I write this, tears are streaming down my face. He whispers in my ear that these tears can't be of sadness, they must be of joy because his mum needs to know he lives on and he is constantly by her side. Chris says he doesn't want to make his beautiful loving mum sad. He wants me to write: 'I LOVE YOU!'

Chapter 7

Where are Kay Docherty and Toni Cavanagh?

Kay Docherty, then aged 16, and Toni Cavanagh, 15, were last seen on Friday, 27 July 1979 at around 7.30 pm. Both girls had left their homes, Kay telling her parents she was babysitting at Toni's house, and Toni that she and Kay were going to the movies with Kay's aunt and uncle. Kay's twin brother Kevin had arranged to pick up his sister from Toni's place at 9.30 pm on his push bike as Kay was afraid of the dark and was not allowed to stay at Toni's overnight. It's believed that the girls planned to hitchhike to the Wollongong CBD to attend a disco, but it's not known whether they got there.

The girls were reported missing on Sunday 29 July. The following week, separate letters from Toni and Kay were posted to their respective parents from the Kings Cross area in Sydney, saying they were staying with friends and would be home soon.

There have been no confirmed sightings of the girls since they were seen alive on Shellharbour Road waiting at a bus stop outside the Warilla Grove Shopping Centre on the evening of 27 July, although there was an unconfirmed sighting in Queensland in 1984.

NAME: Kay Docherty

MISSING SINCE: Friday,
   27 July 1979

LAST SEEN: Warilla, NSW

DATE OF BIRTH: 18
   December 1963

AGE AT DISAPPEARANCE: 16

HEIGHT: 152 cm

BUILD: Medium

HAIR: Ginger-red

EYES: Hazel

COMPLEXION: Fair

CLOTHING: Last seen wearing fawn slacks, a brown floral top and black boots.

Source: Kevin Docherty

NAME: Toni Maree
   Cavanagh

MISSING SINCE: Friday,
   27 July 1979

LAST SEEN: Warilla, NSW

DATE OF BIRTH: 10 January
   1964

AGE AT DISAPPEARANCE: 15

HEIGHT: 147 cm

BUILD: Thin

HAIR: Reddish-blonde

Source: Darren Cavanagh

EYES: Blue

COMPLEXION: Fair

CLOTHING: Last seen wearing a blue blouse, fawn
hooded jacket and white jeans.

◎　◎　◎

In my first book, *Never Alone: A Medium's Journey*, I
wrote about a vision I was shown while I was working
on the backpacker murders. I was taken into a room with
a cream wall. On the wall I could see over 20 Polaroid
photographs of males and females. I later came to realise that
many of the faces on the wall were unsolved missing person
cases. At the time of receiving the vision, I wasn't quite sure
what these faces meant. I wondered if some of the missing
persons were victims who could have been associated with
the backpacker murders and who had not yet been linked to
the case.

I have always thought that Ivan Milat did not always
act alone. Could the other person who was involved in the
murders and abductions of the backpackers be responsible for
the disappearance of Toni and Kay?

I have since come to realise that some of these faces were
people who were in spirit and would seek out my help from
the spirit world. Two of the victims on the wall were the two
teenage girls who went missing from Warilla, New South
Wales.

◎　◎　◎

In 2005, I was asked by Detectives Jeff Little and Catherine Flood if I could assist them with an unsolved murder of a woman named Maria Scott. (I have written about Maria Scott in *Never Alone*.) I met the officers at Port Kembla Police Station and tuned in to some of Maria's belongings. The information that I gave the police was used in part for the preparation of a brief that Jeff Little presented to the coroner.

A few years later Catherine Flood was working at the Illawarra Local Area Command and asked me if I would be able to assist her with an historical missing person's case. Of course I agreed. When I work for the police, I am not given any prior information about the case. That means I can look at each individual case with new eyes and not have any preconceived ideas about what happened.

When I arrived at the Illawarra Local Area Command, which at the time was located at Warilla, I was introduced to some of the other officers there, including Detective Darren Kelly who was also investigating the case with Catherine.

I was taken into a room and asked to tune in to some personal items. I held some pieces of jewellery which were in a small jewellery box. As soon as I held the jewellery I could sense, see and feel the presence of two girls appear before me. The girls felt very familiar to me — I had seen both their faces before. I immediately said that I could see Toni Cavanagh and Kay Docherty appearing before me.

All the officers in the room looked shocked. They asked me to repeat what I had said, so I said the names again. They still looked very shocked. They told me to hold that thought and continue with what I was doing. I would be told more later on.

WHAT I SAW PSYCHICALLY

Once I tuned in to the items belonging to the victims, I began to see visions of two girls and glimpses of their lives. These are the images I was shown:

- I could see a blonde-headed girl and a girl with curly red hair.
- I identified the girls as Toni Maree Cavanagh and Kay Docherty.
- Both these girls had come to me in a vision when I worked on the backpacker murders many years before. They were two of the people in the Polaroids I saw on the cream wall.
- Both girls looked to be around only 15 or 16 years of age.
- I could see the girls in their school uniforms, indicating their ages.
- I was shown the symbol of two fingers being crossed over each other. This is a psychic symbol that to me means close or extremely close. It can also mean twins.
- I was given the word 'twins' and then I could hear the words that they were inseparable.
- Kay was very distraught and she told me that she was worried about her brother. (I later discovered that Kay was a twin. Kay's brother's name is Kevin and they were inseparable.)
- I was shown a pushbike riding past me. When I saw this vision it didn't make any sense to me. The police later told me that Kevin, Kay's twin, rode his push bike to Toni's home at 9.30 pm to pick up Kay and

bring her home because she was frightened of the dark. However Kay wasn't at Toni's house in Martin Street, Warilla, when he arrived and she hasn't been seen since.

- I could hear music.
- One of the girls — who I feel was Toni — told me that they were going to a disco and they wanted to go dancing.
- The blonde girl, who I recognised as Toni, told me that she was the one who convinced the red-headed girl, who I recognised as Kay, that it was okay to go out.
- Kay came across as a very shy girl who looked up to Toni.
- Kay's energy was of a nervous person who worried a lot about doing the right thing.
- I felt that Toni had issues with her parents. If either of the girls thought about running away from home, it would be Toni. I received the impression that she was more streetwise than Kay and at times could be a 'wild child'.
- I felt that Kay was very close to her family and she would never do anything to upset her mother and brother.
- The men involved in the girls' disappearance were known at least to Toni: Kay may have been aware of who they were, but Toni was friendly with the men.
- The men were older and I could see that some of them drove cars. The vehicles I see that are connected to the case in some way are: a Holden EH, a turquoise-green Holden Kingswood HJ and a Holden HR.

- I was given the image of two very strong hands —
  this is a symbol from spirit that the person is
  strong, good with their hands and/or works with
  their hands. I questioned if some of the men had
  apprenticeships and/or worked in the building
  trade.
- I could see Toni would wag school and meet the
  'boys' at an oval next to netball courts. I felt that the
  location was very close to Toni's home. I was given
  the impression that this place was a regular meeting
  point for the young teens.
- I could also see that Toni would meet the 'boys' at
  another location that was behind the girls' school
  and at the back of homes. To access the area you
  would need to walk or drive down a gravel lane way.
- The males looked around 18 to 22 years of age at
  the time the girls went missing. I feel that several
  men were responsible for the girls' disappearance and
  subsequent murder.

Suspect 1: The first man was about 175 to 180 centimetres
tall. He had curly, almost fuzzy, brown/ginger hair down to
his collar, a distinct nose and his eyes were blue. Kay told
me that he had nice white, straight teeth. Suspect 1 was of a
stocky build. He wasn't bad looking, until he got the black
look in his eyes. Kay said that when he is raping her that
the look in his eyes is quite frightening. I felt that the man
was in a school photograph with a brother of one of Toni's
neighbours. He could be an older brother and I saw them at
the netball courts.

Suspect 2: I was shown front-on and side-on mug shots of a second man. He was wearing a checked shirt similar to the Miller brand of western shirts that were popular in the late 1970s and blue jeans. He was a thinner build than the first man and there was something that I kept seeing about his eyes. I felt that his stare is like that of an eagle surveying its prey. The man was around 185 to 190 centimetres tall, of a thin build with a long face. His eyes were beady and blue. His hair was light brown/sandy blond, slightly wavy in a mullet-style haircut (longer at the back, shorter at the sides and layered on the top). He seemed to like to wear a cap or hat and he had a pierced ear. This was not all that common for males in the late 1970s. I felt that this man has re-offended since the murders of the girls and there is some connection to DNA samples. I also saw him in a school photograph. I felt that he could be up to three years older than Kay and Toni.

Kay gave me the names Ron, Ronald, Tim. She told me that Ronald is a surname not a first name and that it is like Ronald McDonald. I am not sure if this is to do with this man's nickname.

Toni was quite smitten with Suspect 2. I see them meeting at the netball courts to have a smoke and join some of the other students wagging school. This seems to be a place to meet and show off.

I also see the men driving their cars and doing doughnuts in a gravel carpark.

I could see that they would meet up near the treeline where a lot of petting would take place. I felt that Toni was confident around the opposite sex.

Kay, on the other hand, was a very quiet and shy girl who wanted to fit into the crowd.

I was also shown a bus stop and felt that the girls had been waiting for a bus.

I was shown the image of a telephone booth, which I felt was located not far from the bus stop. I was given the impression that Toni made a call from the telephone booth to someone she knew, asking to be picked up from the bus stop.

The two girls told me that they were not hitch-hiking, they were picked up by someone known to at least one of the girls.

I felt that the night the girls went missing, Toni had arranged to meet a man known to her and a friend of his and go to a party, and that Kay was unaware of Toni's plans. Kay knew that she would be grounded if she came home too late.

I could see both the girls at the bus stop at Warilla Grove. Kay was not very keen to go but Toni kept egging her on, telling her that they would be back in time for Kevin to pick her up, even though she knew that this was not going to be the case.

I saw that at one stage Kay began to walk back towards her home and Toni ran over to her, grabbed her hand and asked her to stay with her.

I feel that the girls were picked up around 7.30 to 7.45 pm. Toni told Kay that they would just go for a drive and then go to a party for a while, and she said how much fun they were going to have — both girls loved to dance.

The driver of the car told the girls that he needed to pick up a mate at the nearby caravan park near the bridge. He told them that his friend was down for the weekend and staying at his family's caravan. I felt that there was some work connection to the caravan. The caravan was located at the back of the park, right on the water.

I was shown a property that looked like an on-site caravan park located near a bridge situated right beside a lake. This location was connected to the men I saw in my visions. (I feel that the caravan park could now be named Gateway Lifestyle Oaklands and has been converted into a retirement village. The location is off Windang Road, near the bridge. There is a location very similar to this at Lake Illawarra and there is a caravan park similar to this at Gerroa just off Crooked River Road. However, the lake area is not as large as at Lake Illawarra.)

I got the impression that one of the men worked in Sydney or might come from Sydney and then visit a mate on the weekends. The man had a connection to the on-site caravan image I received.

I felt that Toni knew the men and she may have gone to the caravan on prior occasions before her disappearance.

I was shown visions inside the on-site caravan. It looked as though it was used as a weekender or a holiday house. Inside, there was fishing gear and it looked as though it was privately owned or rented on a permanent basis — there were items in the kitchen area that looked like someone lived there.

The caravan had an aluminium annex with windows. It was situated at the back of the caravan park and there was a bridge to the north of the park. Facing the front of the caravan, the water was on the left-hand side and behind the caravan. The caravan's annex area overlooked the water. There could also have been a small aluminium boat connected to the caravan. I could see a white ute that was similar to a 1975 Holden ute.

When they arrived at the caravan, the second man invited the girls to stay and listen to music and have a party there.

Kay did not feel comfortable and told the men that she wanted to leave. The first man told the girls that they would go to the party as they had first planned in order to settle Kay down.

I saw the car leaving the caravan park and then it turning around and heading back down the coast. Toni was in the front passenger's seat and Kay was sitting in the back seat behind the driver with the second man (Suspect 1) beside her.

Kay began to ask the men where they were being taken to. She began to be alarmed when the driver just kept driving the car and didn't answer. The driver kept looking at Kay in the rear-vision mirror, smiling at her with a sick look on his face. Kay began to really worry by this stage but Toni seemed to be quite oblivious to the danger they were in. Toni then shared a cigarette with the driver and didn't seem to be worried at all.

The girls showed me that the police had been looking in the wrong direction. They said that people expected them to have gone in the direction of Wollongong when in fact they were taken south, not north.

I could smell the ocean and I could also see sand, which indicated to me that the girls were taken to a coastal area.

I could see the vehicle the girls and the two men were travelling in was heading south, down past Gerrigong. I was taken through Gerroa and I saw the car cross over the bridge heading towards Seven Mile Beach. The car continued along the road and then I saw it turn left off onto a track that led down to the beach.

I could hear the crunching of the dirt-and-gravel road beneath the car tyres.

I could see the ground littered with leaves and could smell rotting leaves.

The driver then told the girls that he knows a nice secluded spot, where it would be great to watch the submarine races. Toni, who had a crush on the driver, thought this was a good idea. Kay was not at all happy with the decision to go there.

I heard the words 'parking' and 'submarine races'. In the 1970s and early 1980s couples would go 'parking' — park their cars in isolated locations so that they would not be disturbed. The phrase 'submarine races' is a euphemism for making out in a car. This is totally the feeling I was picking up from the girls at the beach location.

I could see a vehicle parked in an isolated area with the lights on. I could hear music blaring out of the car. The music was what would have been played during the late 1970s.

I saw the men in the car getting overly friendly with Toni and Kay. Toni was in the front seat with one man. The man in the back seat was making strong advances towards Kay and she was feeling quite frightened. Toni didn't seem to have the same inhibitions as Kay did. I felt that Toni knew the men in the car so it didn't concern her as much.

I could feel Kay's stress and anxiety. The strongest feeling I was picking up was that she wanted to get away from the dark, isolated area to a safe environment as soon as possible.

I could see that Kay wanted to go home yet Toni kept telling her that everything was alright.

I could see that the men had a bottle of alcohol — the alcohol was intended to relax the girls so they could have their way with them. I was shown images of Bacardi Rum and Southern Comfort. I could see Toni taking a swig from a bottle and begin to laugh. Kay pleaded to be taken home because she was terrified that she would get into trouble with her parents and she was scared of the dark.

I could see Toni beginning to kiss the driver and the man in the back seat trying to grope Kay and kiss her. Kay objected and Toni told her not to be so frigid. Kay began to panic and she struggled with the man and tried to get out of the car.

I felt that there was an altercation between Kay and the man in the back seat. He began to become more and more violent. I could see him grabbing her by the hair and trying to kiss her against her will.

I could see that the headlights of the car were still on and Kay getting out of the car and running in front of the headlights. Kay looks back at Toni and the driver as if she is a startled kangaroo in the headlights.

The car was parked facing the beach and I saw Kay run to the right of the vehicle in the carpark area. I could see her trying to make her way towards the road through the thick bush.

I could see Kay stumble and fall and the man from the back seat catch up to her.

The man threw himself on top of her and began to violently rip off her clothing. The man yelled at Kay angrily, telling her that he knows that she wants it and he began to slap her around the face. The man then raped Kay violently.

Kay tried with all her might to fight him off. I could see that she was hysterical by this time.

Kay showed me that she had scratches on her face from the thick bushes she was running through while she was trying to flee. As I was seeing this vision, I could feel scratches on my own face as if to confirm what I was seeing.

Toni was too caught up with the driver to notice what was going on. The music was still coming from the car so she couldn't hear the commotion. It wasn't until the second man came back to the vehicle that Toni noticed that something was wrong. The man then told Toni that it was now her turn.

Kay tried to put on what remains of her clothing and staggered back, shocked by what the man had done to her. She returned to the car. The second man then pulled out a knife and forced Kay to watch while he raped Toni.

At this point I couldn't seem to see anything. It was as if I was not allowed to witness the horror that the girls were made to endure. I got the feeling that the girls were stabbed to death.

The next image I saw was of one of the men dragging who I believe to be Toni towards the beach. The location was just on the edge of the treeline. There were quite thick scrubby-type trees that look like tea trees and coastal grasses in the area. I could see that the men dug a shallow sandy grave and buried Toni with the sand and the vegetation. I didn't see Toni wearing much clothing — maybe because the men had removed it. I only saw her wearing clothing on the top half of her body.

I felt that Kay was buried closer to the carpark area. I felt that she was in the thicker bushland nearer to the road. The vegetation was different to where Toni was buried.

The message I kept picking up from Kay was that her mum never liked Toni because she thought that she was not the type of girl that Kay should be friends with. Her mother worried that Toni could lead Kay astray.

◎   ◎   ◎

After I stopped tuning in to the items, I was given a copy of a letter that had been received by the Docherty family. The letter was dated 30 July 1979 and was postmarked Darlinghurst, Sydney, on 1 August 1979.

When I held the letter, I was taken back in time. When I was around 13 years old, I had a writing pad exactly the same as the one the letter was written on. I told the police that the writing pad was sold at Woolworths in the 1970s. The paper had the images of a boy and girl watermarked in the background.

Unfortunately, when I tuned in to the letter, I didn't really pick up anything psychically. It almost felt to me that there wasn't much of a connection between Kay and the letter, because I couldn't feel anything. To be honest, I really question if the letter was ever written by Kay. The detectives told me that the handwriting on the letter was verified by the family as being Kay's. However, I have since spoken to Kevin and he said that both he and his mother questioned whether the letter was written by Kay. Kevin said that the writing was not as neat and tidy as the family remembered Kay's handwriting to be.

To this day this letter baffles me. For the murderer/s to get Kay to write a letter and then the letter to be sent from the Kings Cross/Darlinghurst area makes you think that the

Kay Docherty's mother Jean Docherty and twin brother Kevin. Jean has since passed away not knowing what happened to her daughter.
Source: Kevin Docherty

girls' murders were premeditated. This doesn't fit in with my visions. I question whether the men had planned to kill the girls or it was a sexual attack that went wrong. I wish that I was given more psychic information in connection to the letter to try and make sense of what happened.

I was then shown a Google map of the area that I thought could be where the girls were taken and murdered. I was very drawn to Seven Mile Beach, just south of Gerrigong. On the map I could see there were three significant bush tracks that lead down to the beach.

The officers asked if I would take a drive down to the area that I had seen in my visions in the hope I could identify an area that could be searched.

Before going to Seven Mile Beach, we visited Kay's home. There I was introduced to a man who I felt I had met before. When we shook hands, I realised that I was standing before Kay Docherty's twin brother Kevin. It was quite surreal to be meeting an older version of the young man I had seen riding a pushbike in my visions. I was also introduced to Kay's mother Jean. I could feel the pain and anguish she had endured for so many years, not knowing where her beautiful daughter was.

The wonderful thing about meeting family members of the missing is that I am able to share messages with them from their loved ones in spirit. I spoke briefly to both Jean and Kevin about Kay and asked Kevin about some of the images that I had seen while I was tuning in at the police station.

Kevin told me about that night when he had gone to pick up his sister from Toni's place only to find that she wasn't there. I could see the pain in his eyes when he described it to me. Meeting the family made me more determined to try and help the officers find out what happened to the two girls.

When we left the Dochertys, we drove past the Cavanagh home to give me an idea of the distance between the girls' houses and the route that they would have used to get there. We also visited the bus stop where the girls were seen waiting. I was also shown the location of the now-removed telephone booth. Both locations fitted in with my visions — I had seen the girls at a bus stop and then Toni making a phone call from a telephone booth.

Next I was taken to another significant place I had seen in my visions. The detectives were well aware of both locations I had seen. On this occasion we visited the carpark situated at the back of Lake Illawarra High School which the girls had attended.

Apparently, Toni frequently met male friends who owned cars there after school. When we arrived at the oval carpark, I felt as if I was taken back in time. I could see Toni speaking with the young men who were sitting in cars. I felt that the two men had possibly frequented this area prior to the girls' disappearance. One of the men could be a local, the other could come from Sydney or worked in Sydney. There was a very strong sense of familiarity with the location. What I found most interesting about it was that I didn't feel Kay's energy there. I wondered if this was because it was mainly Toni who came to this place, not Kay.

I found it very helpful to be able to physically visit the location to get my bearings and to piece together the psychic information I had seen at the police station.

The police said that they knew about the netball courts and they were aware that Toni would also visit this location to meet up with male friends who were known to do burnouts in the carpark.

The netball courts are located on Johnston Street which is the nearest cross-street from Toni's home. We left the oval and drove down to Gerringong and then onto the location at Gerroa near Seven Mile Beach. As we drove down past the town of Gerroa and crossed the bridge on Crooked River Road, I felt I was in the right area. I told the officers it was important to drive down each of the three beach access roads because they were all within a few kilometres of each other.

Twins Kay and Kevin Docherty with their parents. Source: Kevin Docherty

We turned off and drove down the first access road and I got out of the car. I felt that we were close but something just didn't feel right. When we drove down the second access road, the place fitted more of what I saw in my visions. I got out of the car and had a walk around. This area felt right.

As I really wanted to be sure which area felt the strongest to me psychically, I asked if we could visit the third access road. This location was definitely not right.

We decided to go back to the second spot. It had the strongest connection to my visions and to the girls. Once there, I got out of the car and tuned in further to the girls. They began to share with me what had happened to them on the night of their murders in 1979.

It was now 2009 and the vegetation around us had changed significantly, and so had the road and parking area close to the beach. There were newly installed public toilets, which I knew changed the look of the site. However, the feeling was still very strong for me.

As I walked towards the beach, I could smell the same smells that I had at the local area command when I had tuned in to the jewellery. I could smell the ocean, I could smell the same rotting leaves and I suddenly heard music playing in my ears. The sandy area and the type of vegetation were correct so I felt that we were in the right place.

We walked around for a time and discussed the options of returning later to do a police search. I told the officers that I was open to the idea and that they just needed to let me know when they arranged a date and time so that I could make myself available.

During the visions of the girls fleeing, I was given a really good look at the men's faces. When we returned to the local area command, I did two identikits (known as comfits) with Detective Darren Kelly of what each perpetrator looked like.

I have previously worked with a police artist in Western Australia to do an identikit of the Claremont serial killer. In that instance, I was able to work with the artist and he made the facial composite directly on the computer and I was able to change the features instantly until I was happy with what I saw.

Doing the comfits in New South Wales was a very different experience. We did the images by using a book with a myriad of facial features to create the faces. For each part of a person's face there was a different section with numbered facial parts. I had to choose the facial parts I felt fitted my visions best. The hardest part of working this way was that I didn't see the final image of the faces

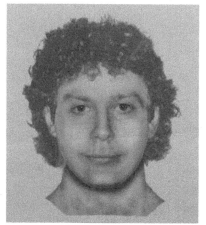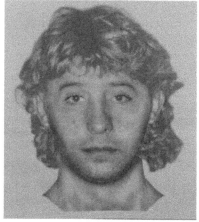

The comfit images I did with police of the two men who I saw in my visions involved in the disappearance of Toni Maree Cavanagh and Kay Docherty. Suspect 1 (left) and Suspect 2 (right). Source: Kevin Docherty

until a few weeks later. Thankfully, when the elements were composited together, the images fitted those of the men I had seen in my visions. My only hope is that someone someday will recognise these men so that the truth will come out about what happened to the girls on the night of their disappearance.

SUSPECT DETAILS

Suspect 1

GENDER: Male

AGE: 18-22 in 1979

HEIGHT: 175-180 cm

BUILD: Medium

HAIR: Dark ginger

COMPLEXION: Fair

OTHER: Caucasian

Suspect 2

GENDER: Male

AGE: 18-22 in 1979

HEIGHT: 185-190 cm

BUILD: Thin

HAIR: Sandy blonde

COMPLEXION: Fair

OTHER: Caucasian, earring in left ear

◎ ◎ ◎

A few weeks later I received a phone call from Catherine Flood, letting me know the date and time the area I had pinpointed was being searched.

The date was Thursday, 25 March 2010 and, to be honest, I was excited yet very nervous about what we might or might not find. I arrived at the search area at around 11 am. Catherine and Kevin Docherty were there and I was introduced to two officers from the New South Wales Police Force Dog Unit who had two 'cadaver-trained' dogs with them. Also known as 'human-remains detection' dogs, these animals have been trained specifically to smell decomposition, which means they can locate body parts, tissue, blood and bone. This was a very interesting moment for me as I had always wanted to work with members from this unit.

When we met, the dog-unit officers, Leading Senior Constable David Cole and Sergeant Roger Mayer, were not aware what my role was. When Roger asked me what connection I had to the case, I quietly said that I was a psychic. He just looked at me, rolled his eyes and said that he didn't believe in that sort of thing. Roger said that although he was a sceptic, he still had an open mind to things and he said he would wait to see what happened during the search.

I really began to feel the pressure and hoped that I was going to be of assistance, at least in some small way, during the day ahead. We discussed my feelings about the case and the visions I saw. I explained what I was looking for.

The search began. Dave gave me a reel of hot pink surveyors' tape (also known as flagging tape) and asked me to go into the bush area and tie bits of the tape on search areas that I felt drawn to.

I was extremely lucky to work with these two officers. The information they gave me about how they conduct their searches was an invaluable asset for me as a psychic working on these types of cases. The way Roger and Dave worked with their cadaver dogs made me look at my surroundings in a very different way. Being able to determine if the earth around you has been disturbed, and looking to see if something has been covered up by a human or simply has been left untouched by nature, helped me to understand what to pay attention to while we were in the bush looking for the girls' remains.

The dogs and their officers worked in unison. Before the dogs did a run-through search of the areas I identified, metal probes were poked into the ground at significant points of interest. The dogs were then led to each hole and they would sniff the area to ascertain if there was anything of interest.

As I was walking around in the bush area between the road and the beach, I found multiple items. A woman's leather handbag, which had been in the bush for some time, was full of personal items, including make-up, a hairbrush and mirror, but no identification. I hoped that it might be something connected to the case but Kevin did not recognise the bag. Then I found a backpack which contained empty medal cases and trophies. I just wished that I could locate things connected to the case and not discarded stolen items. Finding these items indicated to me that people had frequented the bush area in the past. I felt that it could be a hopeful sign that the girls had been taken to this place.

I continued to mark off the bush area. It was about 28 degrees Celsius and there wasn't a breath of wind in the air. The heat was quite stifling. I came across a big patch of cabbage tree palms and began to mark off the area as a significant search area. Suddenly, an extremely strong breeze raced through the trees. The sound was so loud all I could hear was the rustling and whooshing of the leaves and foliage around me.

I became overcome with psychic visions and very disorientated. I felt as if Kay had taken me over and I was being chased. I wanted to run and get the hell out of the bush because the energy in there was extremely unpleasant. This is one of the strangest experiences I have ever had while doing a search for a case.

Roger yelled out to see if I was okay, but I couldn't hear him because of the noise of the wind. He came over and the wind suddenly stopped. I explained that I felt that I had Kay with me and that something odd had gone on near the cabbage tree palms.

Roger said he would come back to the location with me and let his dog Jeff do a run through of the area and see if he had any reaction. As we got close to the cabbage tree palms where I had placed the search tape, the winds just as suddenly began to rush and whirl around us. If we spread out and were further apart the winds would stop, but when we came closer together near the palms the winds would suddenly erupt into action.

Roger said that he had not had this type of experience happen before. Both of us didn't really know what was going on. However, we both felt that there was a definite energy shift at this location. We hoped that this was an indication that we may have been close to finding one or both of the missing girls.

Dave was searching the area along the bush track closer to the beach. Between the two cadaver dog officers, quite a large area of the bush, carpark and beach track was searched. When the dogs pick up something, they react by either sitting or indicating that they have picked up a scent.

I was extremely disappointed that we didn't find anything that day. The officers decided to return to the location in a few weeks, based on the fact that the initial search was conducted late in the afternoon and more light hours were required to complete a thorough search of the area. They both agreed that the beach wasn't called Seven Mile Beach for nothing.

The girls had been missing for 20 years so there were a lot of things to consider. Roger and Dave explained that the topography of the coastal land would change due to the wind, the vegetation dropping on the forest floor, as well as the movement of the sand.

Before we left the area Roger admitted that initially he had been a skeptic about working with a psychic, but by the end of the day he had changed his mind. As he said, we had both experienced something by the cabbage tree palms. What that was he couldn't say, but whatever it was had made the hairs on his arms stand up — he had had a definite reaction.

It was disappointing that we didn't come up with any new information about the girls. I felt very strongly that I was in or around the area. I just needed to hone in my psychic skills better to find their remains. One of the most frustrating things about working on a case psychically is that, when I tune in, I only receive fragments of what happened to the victims. It is like watching a movie and only being shown little snippets of information and not the complete story.

People have often asked me why I can't just say that the person is at a certain address or location. I wish that I could see an exact map with a big X on the spot and hear that 'I am here.'

Roger and Dave both said that the search was not a waste of time. We had eliminated a large area, so we knew that Kay and Toni were not in the area we had searched. What baffled me most was what Roger and I experienced near the cabbage tree palms. I have never felt that type of energy before. At least I know it wasn't my imagination — Roger, an experienced and once sceptical police officer, admitted that he couldn't explain the experience either.

⊚　⊚　⊚

On Tuesday, 4 May 2010 at around 9.30 am, I returned to the location with Catherine Flood, Dave Cole and his dog Oscar. We did an extensive search of the area and unfortunately found nothing connected to the girls. It is disappointing that my visions matched up with other police intelligence connected to the case, yet we still haven't got any closer to finding the two missing girls.

⊚　⊚　⊚

A second coronial inquest before New South Wales Deputy State Coroner Geraldine Beattie was held in August 2013. Ms Beattie said, based on the information presented to the court, she was satisfied that there was no reliable evidence to conclude Kay and Toni were still alive. 'I find that both girls are deceased, by criminal means, at an unknown location in the days after their [1979] disappearance,' she said. 'What I can't determine is how their deaths came about.'

※ ※ ※

The most unfortunate thing about this case is that Jean Docherty, Kay's mother, passed away on 5 March 2014 without knowing the truth about what happened to her daughter. I am sorry that I wasn't able to provide the answers that Jean was looking for. I hope that someone, somewhere, may have some new information about what happened to Kay and Toni on that fateful night.

I hope that the identikits I did with the police will be released in an attempt for new evidence to come to the surface.

※ ※ ※

I wish to thank Catherine Flood, Darren Kelly, Roger Mayer and Dave Cole for allowing me to work with them on the case. It has been a privilege to have been able to work with such talented and dedicated officers. I feel that it is very important that the public know how hard these officers have worked to bring an outcome to this case. Too often people think that a cold case is simply put aside and filed away and forgotten. Catherine Flood has done her utmost to explore all avenues with this cold case.

To the Docherty and Cavanagh families, I hope that one day you will find the closure you so rightly deserve.

The comfit images were supplied by Kevin Docherty.

Acknowledgements

The journey to start and finalise this book has been an arduous task, to say the least. The beautiful people in this book have been the reason to carry on. As a psychic medium I have experienced so much pain and trauma of the victims that at times I have questioned why I continued to write about the victims' experiences and pain.

On the other side of the coin, I have also experienced the privilege and trust of the victims who allowed me to be their voices from the other side. All the victims in this book want you to know that they were ordinary people, just like you and me, whose lives were lost at the hand of another.

All of these beautiful beings are still connected to their loved ones, even though they are now on the other side. My one hope in life is that by writing this book, one day at least one of their families will find closure.

To the dedicated officers who have spent a large part of their careers working on these cases selflessly, I totally commend you. Too often the public criticise the work of the officers who dedicate their lives to find closure. I totally understand that once you engage on working on a case that it can become part of your life. All the officers who I have worked with on the cases in this book are my greatest inspiration. They are shining lights and they should be very proud of their efforts. I feel privileged to have been given the opportunity to be able to contribute in a small way on their cases.

To my family, I love you all more than life itself. I can't thank you all enough for putting up with me being stuck at the computer writing or going out on location to assist on cases. You are all amazing and patient to put up with me. I thank you for being a part of my life.

To my gorgeous manager and dear friend Richard Martin, thank you for being there with me along my roller-coaster ride. You know how amazing I think you are.

A huge thank you to Lisa and the amazing team at Rockpool Publishing. You have helped my dreams become a reality.

My final wish for this book is for the victims and their families to find a voice and to hopefully find closure.

Sources

1. Working with the Cadaver Dog Unit

murderpedia.org/female.A/a/abrahams-kristi.htm

www.readersdigest.com.au/magazine/The-Hunt-to-Find-Kiesha-p4.asp

www.smh.com.au/national/duty-of-care-what-happened-to-kiesha-20130825-2skl1.html

www.smh.com.au/nsw/kristi-abrahams-jailed-for-at-least-16-years-over-murder-of-daughter-kiesha-weippeart-20130718-2q5td.html

http://guides.sl.nsw.gov.au/content.php?pid=242811&sid=4001783

www.austlii.edu.au/cgi-bin/sinodisp/au/cases/nsw/NSWSC/2013/729

www.austlii.edu.au/cgi-bin/sinodisp/au/cases/nsw/NSWSC/2013/952

www.mako.org.au/Robert-Smith-Kiesha-Weippeart's-step-father-Robert-Smith-jailed.html

2. The Murders at Murphy's Creek

www.courts.qld.gov.au/__data/assets/pdf_file/0015/202245/cif-evans-wj-wilson-lr-20130628.pdf

www.9now.com.au/60-minutes/2014

www.thechronicle.com.au/news/murphys-creek-nurses-murders-dark-chapter-our-hist/2755533/#/0

www.thechronicle.com.au/news/violent-gang-known-abducting-women-inquest-told/1824475/#/0

www.thechronicle.com.au/topic/murphys-creek-murders/

www.couriermail.com.au/news/queensland/state-coroner-finds-no-one-will-stand-trial-for-brutal-murder-of-two-nurses-at-murphys-creek-in-1974/news-story/6690731a0800c65491983f5945c00850

www.brisbanetimes.com.au/queensland/abducted-raped-bashed-and-
    left-for-dead-20130619-2oist.html
www.tvtonight.com.au/2014/02/60-minutes-mar-2.html
Eric Wilson: *The Echo of Silent Screams* and *The Gold Coast
Hitchhike Murders*

3. What Happened to Bob Chappell?

www.abc.net.au/news/2014-08-20/fresh-bid-to-have-bob-chappell-
    murder-case-reviewed/5683336
www.australianmissingpersonsregister.com/BobChappell.htm
www.magistratescourt.tas.gov.au/about_us/coroners/
    coronialfindings/c/chappell,_robert_adrian_-_2014_tascd_04
http://tasmaniantimes.com/index.php/article/sue-neill-fraser-two-
    views-of-her-guilt
http://tasmaniantimes.com/index.php?/pr-article/what-really-
    happened-to-bob-chappell/
Shadow of a Doubt, documentary directed by Eve Ash

4. The Disappearances of Dorothy Davis and Kerry Whelan

murderpedia.org/male.B/b/burrell-bruce.htm
www.smh.com.au/nsw/bernie-whelan-dies-with-mystery-of-wifes-
    disappearance-unsolved-20160303-gna6dn.html
www.australianmissingpersonsregister.com/Whelan.htm
guides.sl.nsw.gov.au/content.php?pid=242811&sid=2189487
http://netk.net.au/NSW/Burrell5.asp
www.australianmissingpersonsregister.com/DottieDavis.htm
http://guides.sl.nsw.gov.au/content.php?pid=242811&sid=2189486

5. Who Shot Shane Barker?

www.themercury.com.au/news/tasmania/shane-barker-police-
    surprised-by-calculated-shooting-of-unlikely-victim-gunned-
    down-at-his-home/news-story/574208e6224830240f96f249834e
    ea19
www.abc.net.au/news/2016-08-30/fresh-police-search-at-campbell-
    town-over-shane-barker-murder/7797890
www.youtube.com/watch?v=vOGzadz6CYA

6. *P.S. I Love You:* The Chris Noble Story

www.canberratimes.com.au/act-news/at-the-time-of-rozelle-blast-chris-noble-sends-a-final-text-message-of-love-20140913-10gid1.html

www.smh.com.au/nsw/adeel-khan-found-guilty-of-murder-following-rozelle-explosion-and-fire-20160601-gp8xdi.html

7. Where are Kay Docherty and Toni Cavanagh?

www.illawarramercury.com.au/story/1718774/warilla-cold-case-family-can-finally-grieve-kay-and-toni/

www.illawarramercury.com.au/story/4091857/did-these-men-kill-warilla-schoolgirls-kay-and-toni/

www.australianmissingpersonsregister.com/KayDocherty.htm

Other products by Debbie...

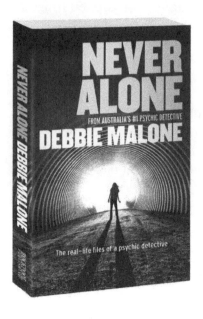

Never Alone:
The real-life files of a
psychic detective

ISBN: 978-1-92542-954-1

This book takes readers on the roller-coaster ride of Debbie's journey, from receiving confirmation of her capacities after a miscarriage at the age of twenty-eight, filming with ghosts for the TV show Scream Test and becoming an adept spirit photographer, to volunteering her services to the police on high-profile cases, including the backpacker murders in Belanglo State Forest and the Claremont murders in Perth.

Available at all good bookstores or online at
www.rockpoolpublishing.com.au